SIGHT LOSS

The Essential Guide

Need
— 2 —
Know

**Antonia Chitty &
Victoria Dawson**

Sight Loss – The Essential Guide is also available in accessible formats for people with any degree of sight loss. The large print edition and ebook (with accessibility features enabled) are available from Need2Know. Please let us know if there are any special features you require and we will do our best to accommodate your needs.

First published in Great Britain in 2011 by
Need2Know
Remus House
Coltsfoot Drive
Peterborough
PE2 9JX
Telephone 01733 898103
Fax 01733 313524
www.need2knowbooks.co.uk

Need2Know is an imprint of Bonacia Ltd.
www.forwardpoetry.co.uk

Contents

Introduction

Are you one of the 1.8 million people in the UK affected by sight loss? Or is a close friend or family member experiencing worsening vision? Do you work with people with partial sight? Whatever your position, this practical guide is here to help.

Sight loss is something that happens to many of us as we age. Losing your sight is stressful and confusing. You can find yourself visiting a number of professionals who may talk in jargon, and afterwards sit at home wondering exactly what is happening to your sight. Don't panic. There are simple things you can do right away to make your life easier. For example, if you're struggling to read this, try sitting in better light. That's just one of the things that might help. This book is packed with further practical ideas to make everyday life easier.

If you're confused about the difference between blindness and partial sight, chapter 1 will help. In chapter 2 we look at why people's sight can get worse as they age, and in chapters 3 to 6 you can read about the leading causes of sight loss:

- Macular degeneration.
- Glaucoma.
- Cataract.
- Diabetic retinopathy.

For each of these conditions we'll clearly explain the problem, how it is detected and how it can be treated.

Sight loss can be isolating too – suddenly you may feel less able to get out and about. Your favourite leisure activities may become increasingly difficult, but there are ways to help you start enjoying life again and feeling like you can cope. In chapter 7 we look at the help available to get out and about. There are organisations in your area that are there to help you feel more confident when you are walking down the street: this chapter tells you about mobility training and more.

If cooking and cleaning has become a struggle for you, in chapter 8 we look at how you can cope better at home. By using better lighting and simple gadgets, your day-to-day life can become much more manageable. In chapter 9 we focus on getting help with finances. A little extra money can make it much easier to get on with your life and this chapter explains about benefits, grants and other ways to help your money meet your needs. In chapter 10 we look at helpful ideas if you are experiencing sight loss alongside another disability.

Read on to get practical tips and a better understanding of your eye problems.

Thanks for help with this book go to:

- Brian Little, BSc MA FHEA FRCS FRCOphth, consultant ophthalmologist training director, Cataract Service, NHS Moorfields Eye Hospital.

- Som Prasad, MS FRCSEd FRCOphth FACS, consultant ophthalmologist, Wirral University Teaching Hospital.

- Dee Beach, rehabilitation officer, Guide Dogs.

- Stephen Kill, rehabilitation office, SeeAbility.

- Nick Rumney, MScOptom FCOptom FAAO FBCLA, BBR Optometry Ltd.

Sight Loss – The Essential Guide is also available in large print format, please visit the website (www.need2knowbook.co.uk) for more information.

Disclaimer

This book is for general information about sight loss. Anyone with health concerns should consult their GP or healthcare professional in the first instance. This book can be used alongside professional medical advice but does not replace it – always check with your GP or healthcare professional before acting on any of the medical information in this book.

Chapter One

About Sight Loss

Are you concerned that your sight is not as good as it used to be? Or do you think that a friend or family member may have problems seeing things? If so, you're not alone. There are 1.8 million people in the UK with some level of sight loss.

Visiting an eye specialist is the first step to finding out about your sight loss. Visit an optometrist or ophthalmic optician: you can usually find a local practice on every high street. They can check your sight and see if your vision can be improved by glasses. An optometrist will also check the health of your eyes and can detect signs of eye disease. Many eye diseases are treatable, but bear in mind that the sooner some conditions are treated, the easier it is to preserve your sight – so don't delay making an appointment.

This chapter will cover:

- Who can help you look after your eyes.

- Some practical tips to help you see better right now.

- More information about what sight loss means.

Who can help?

Optometrist

An optometrist or ophthalmic optician looks for signs of eye disease and assesses your eyes to see if they would benefit from glasses.

Your GP

If your glasses are up to date yet you are still concerned about your eyesight, you can talk to your GP. They will act as the gatekeeper for your health and can refer you to the right professionals for the help you need.

Ophthalmologist

An ophthalmologist is a doctor who specialises in eye problems. If your GP or optometrist spots something which needs more investigation, you will be referred to hospital to see an ophthalmologist.

Rehabilitation officer

'Every adult should get their eyes tested every two years. If you are worried about your sight, you don't need to wait: book a test right away.'

A rehabilitation officer can help you learn new ways of doing things and help you cope emotionally. They will talk through what you need and come up with a plan to meet those needs. You may find one via your local social care department, your local society for people with sight loss or via your GP.

Going for an eye test

Every adult should get their eyes tested every two years. If you are worried about your sight, you don't need to wait: book a test right away. During an eye test the optometrist can check the health of your eyes as well as your level of vision and whether you need new glasses to help you see better.

What happens during the test

An eye examination contains a number of routine parts.

- Your history – the optometrist will ask about your medical history, medication and whether anyone in your family has eye problems. You should tell the optometrist about any difficulties you have with focusing, headaches or other problems.

- Checking your eye health – the optometrist will shine a bright light close to your eyes to check the inside and outside of the eyes for signs of disease.

- Checking your vision – the optometrist will ask you to read letters on a chart and use different lenses to see how much your vision can be improved for distant and near objects.

- Checking how your eyes work together – the optometrist will ask you to look at a letter or object and will then cover one eye at a time to see how well your eyes work together.

- Checking the pressure inside your eyes – your eye is filled with fluid and sometimes the pressure of the fluid rises, which can cause sight loss. The optometrist should check the pressure inside your eyes at every test once you reach the age of 40. This can be done with a machine that blows a little puff of air on the eye or by resting a small probe on the eye.

- Checking your field of vision – the optometrist will check how well you can see at the edge of your field of vision using a test that flashes faint spots of light.

- At the end of the test – occasionally, the optometrist may ask you to come back for a repeat test, after using some eye drops. These drops relax the eye muscles and let the optometrist see more clearly inside your eyes to get a more accurate result. The drops may sting at first and can cause blurred vision for a short while. If it is a bright day, you may want to bring sunglasses with you as you may find the drops make your eyes more sensitive to glare for an hour or so. Do ask someone else to drive you home after eye drops like this.

If you need glasses, the optometrist will write you a prescription. It will look something like this:

Patient's name	Jane Smith	Date	5 January 2011
Right eye distance vision	+2.00/+1.50x180	Left eye distance vision	+2.25/+1.25x175
Near vision add	+2.00		+2.00
Signed	An Optician	Recommended retest	2 years

You may be long-sighted, which is also known as 'hyperopia'. On the spectacle prescription, this would be shown as a plus (+) sign at the start of each line of figures. If you are long-sighted, you have to work harder to focus on close objects. If there is a minus (-) sign at the start of the prescription, you are short-sighted and will struggle to see distant objects.

The second figure for each eye, after the slash, shows how astigmatic (or rugby ball shaped) your eyes are. Correcting this with glasses can make things clearer at all distances.

And over the age of 40, almost everyone starts to find it hard to see small objects close up. The near vision addition will help with this.

If an eye test shows that you have a possible problem with your eyes, your optometrist will write a letter to your GP who can refer you to see a hospital eye specialist. Make an appointment with your GP to talk about referral to see an ophthalmologist (eye specialist) at the eye hospital.

'If an eye test shows that you have a possible problem with your eyes, your optometrist will write a letter to your GP who can refer you to see a hospital eye specialist.'

Make the most of your sight

There are three simple principles that will make your life much easier if your sight is poor. Try to make things:

- Bigger – the larger something is, the easier it is to see. If you struggle using the phone, check out places like the RNIB shop. You can find phones with large numbers on large buttons, as well as watches with large, clear numbers, easy-to-see kitchen scales and large print games like scrabble. A magnifier makes things bigger and easier to use too. Surprisingly, there are techniques to learn to make the most out of any magnifier, so it is always worth getting professional advice from an optician or low vision specialist at your hospital eye department.

- Bolder – bold lines are easier to see than faint ones, so to make it easier at home you could buy some black marker pens with a medium or thick nib. This will allow you to read and write notes more easily. If you struggle with navigating around your home, think about whether you can use bold black or white lines to help. A contrast strip on the edge of a stair can make it stand out, and contrasting tape on hard corners can save you from knocking yourself each time you pass.

- Brighter – if you find something hard to see, better light will always help. Try changing your light bulbs for more powerful ones, and add in an extra reading lamp that can shine over your shoulder when you look at a book. Look at the places where you find things difficult to see and think about whether you could add in extra light.

At the hospital

If you are referred to the hospital to see an ophthalmologist, they will carry out a thorough examination of your eyes. Your level of vision may be checked, just the same as when you visit the optometrist.

The ophthalmologist will look inside your eyes with a bright light and is likely to use drops to dilate or widen your pupils to get a better view. This will cause your vision to be blurry for a short while afterwards, so you should take someone with you who can drive you home.

You may have further tests, depending on the particular problem that is being investigated. There are a number of things that could be causing your sight loss, and common causes of sight loss are covered later on in this book.

More help

If you have low vision that cannot be remedied with glasses, medication or an operation, there are still lots of things that can help you make the most of the sight that you have. At the hospital, you should be put in touch with a low vision specialist who can assess you and recommend magnifiers or other technology to help.

Ask if you can be assessed by a rehabilitation officer who can help with practical adaptations to your home. You can get in touch via your GP, your local social care department or local society for people with sight problems. You should also ask about mobility training to help you get about independently. You'll find out more about this in chapters 7 and 8.

The hospital may also be able to point you towards local support groups and a contact at your local authority's social care department (this used to be known as social services). The social care department may be able to assist with equipment to make day-to-day life easier, including speaking clocks and telephones with larger numbers.

Measuring sight

We rarely think about how sight is measured, but if you are losing your sight it can help to understand a little about how professionals measure your vision and some of the terms they will use.

Visual acuity

Visual acuity measures the size of an object you can see. If you have visited an optometrist, you will remember the test chart of black, high contrast letters with a white background on the wall. This is called a Snellen chart. In the UK, the charts are hung at a standard 6 metres from the person viewing them, or more often 3 metres reflected in a mirror.

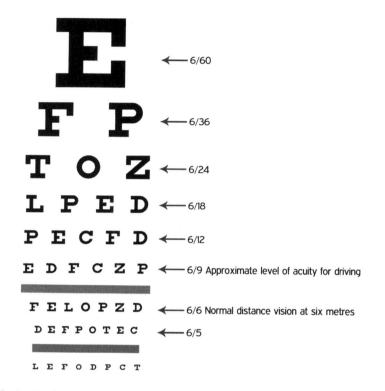

E ← 6/60

F P ← 6/36

T O Z ← 6/24

L P E D ← 6/18

P E C F D ← 6/12

E D F C Z P ← 6/9 Approximate level of acuity for driving

F E L O P Z D ← 6/6 Normal distance vision at six metres

D E F P O T E C ← 6/5

L E F O D P C T

Note: this Snellen chart is not to scale and should not be used to measure your sight.

'If you think of blindness, you may think of someone who can see nothing at all. In fact, most people who are 'blind' have some sight.'

Most people are able to achieve 6/6 vision. This usually means at six metres they can see the letters on the last but one line of a Snellen chart (see diagram). Some charts have a smaller 6/5 line, and some have a 6/4 line too, so this will vary depending on your practitioner's equipment.

Someone with 6/9 vision can stand 6 metres away from a chart and just about see a 6/9 letter on a chart (see diagram). The number plate test when learning to drive, where you're asked to read a number plate from a distance of about six metres, just about equates to approximately 6/9 to 6/12 vision.

If you think of blindness, you may think of someone who can see nothing at all. In fact, most people who are 'blind' have some sight. There is an official definition for the level of sight you need to have to be classed as blind and the level to be partially sighted when wearing glasses. However, these terms are no longer used: the preferred terms are 'severely visually impaired' or 'visually impaired'.

- Visual impairment (partial sight) is defined as visual acuity of less than 6/60 in the better-seeing eye (assuming full visual field).

- Severe visual impairment (blindness) is defined as visual acuity of less than 3/60 in the better-seeing eye (assuming full field).

- People with a reduced visual field (see below) can also be certified as severely visually impaired or visually impaired even if the visual acuity is better than the above.

Contrast

As described above, visual acuity measures the size of object you can see and the degree of contrast you can see, such as dense black on a white background. Many sight problems, however, are due to problems with low contrast objects. Your ability to see low contrast, objects declines with age and conditions like cataracts can cause particular problems with contrast.

Contrast sensitivity can be measured. There are specific test charts that show shapes or letters with different levels of contrast but there is no single standardised test. In practice, this test does not happen routinely.

Visual field

As well as measuring how well you can see looking straight ahead, there are also tests to assess your peripheral vision or visual field. If you focus on an object straight ahead, you will also be aware of everything else to the left and right, above and below the object you are looking at. This is your visual field.

In a condition like glaucoma, it is the central visual field that is affected first, causing patches of low vision that you are unlikely to be aware of as one eye compensates for the other. Other conditions such as retinitis pigmentosa or stroke may cause visual field loss in the periphery. A visual field test will map out areas of good, moderate and poor vision for each eye. Your eye specialist can then assess progress of disease or effectiveness of treatment in

'If you focus on an object straight ahead, you will also be aware of everything else to the left and right, above and below the object you are looking at. This is your visual field.'

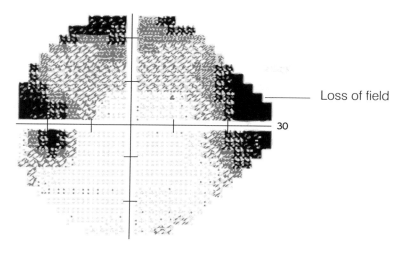

Loss of field

30

preserving your vision. Some visual field tests are conducted to see if there is a possibility of loss of field (screening) and some are done to measure known loss (full threshold). See the diagram above to see what a visual field map looks like.

Practically, a loss of visual field can make it dangerous to drive as you may not see hazards approaching from the right or left. You may need to take more care to turn your head and listen carefully while crossing the road to ensure that you spot oncoming vehicles.

If you have a very restricted visual field, this can also allow you to register as blind or partially sighted, even if your central visual acuity is as good as 6/18 or better.

Registering your sight loss

It is possible to register as blind or partially sighted with your local authority. This can help you get certain benefits and help with travel. The benefits of registering as blind or partially sighted include discounts on rail travel through the Disabled Person's Railcard, access to the Blue Badge Scheme and discounted TV license fees. Anyone registered blind also gets a tax allowance worth £1,890, whatever your age or income (at the time of going to press). You can also get free NHS sight tests: even if you have sight problems, your eyes still need a regular check-up and you may continue to benefit from an up-to-date spectacle prescription.

Before registering, you need to speak to your ophthalmologist. If they think you qualify, they will complete a certificate of vision impairment and send it to your local authority's social care department. There is more advice about finances in chapter 9.

Advice for carers

If your friend or family member is worried about their sight, there are lots of ways you can help. To start with:

- You could go with them for an eye test at the optician.

- Help them improve lighting around the house to reduce the risk of falls and generally make life a bit easier for your loved one.

- Mark trip hazards around the house or garden with tape in a contrasting colour.

Quick action checklist

- Make an appointment with your optometrist or GP to get your eyes tested and, if needed, a referral to an ophthalmologist at hospital or low vision services.

- Call the RNIB helpline (0303 123 9999) – they will give you information on practical and emotional support and help you find more sources of help locally.

- Ask a relative or friend to walk around the house with you. Think about where you need to make things bigger, bolder and brighter.

- Get in touch with your ophthalmologist (if you have been referred to one) to find out about registering as blind or partially sighted, or ask for a referral to the low vision service or rehabilitation officer.

Summing Up

- If you're worried about your sight, the first thing to do is to get your eyes checked. If you haven't had an eye test for some time, visit your local optometrist to see if you need new spectacles or advice on lighting. They can also detect signs of eye disease.

- If you are struggling at home, can you make things bigger, bolder or brighter? There are some things that you can do yourself, but you can also ask your eye specialist to put you in touch with your local low vision service and rehabilitation officer.

Chapter Two

Sight Loss as You Get Older

If your sight is not as good as it used to be, you're not alone. RNIB research predicts that by 2050, the numbers of people with partial sight and blindness in the UK will double to nearly four million people, and most people find their sight worsening as they get older.

The leading causes of sight loss are all age related. In this chapter, you can find out a little bit about:

- The causes of sight loss.
- How to protect your eyes.
- Where to get help and support if your sight is failing.

Causes of sight loss

Age-related macular degeneration (AMD) is the leading cause of sight loss. It damages the vision at the centre of the eye, causing problems with reading, writing and other close work. However, side vision is retained, which helps when moving around. There are different types of macular degeneration. Wet macular degeneration is less common but there are more treatment possibilities. There are also other less common but more specific macular problems such as macular holes. See chapter 3 for more details.

Glaucoma is a degeneration of a particular type of nerve cell that results in a loss of peripheral vision and ultimately all eyesight, if untreated. There are two forms of glaucoma: open angle, which is painless and may be treated with eye drops to reduce internal fluid pressure in the eye, and closed angle, which may be painful as a result of increased internal fluid pressure and may require surgery to reduce it.

Glaucoma can be detected as part of a routine eye test. Untreated, glaucoma can cause you to lose parts of your peripheral vision, making it hard to get around as the disease progresses. Central vision is less likely to be affected until very late stages in the disease. Glaucoma runs in families and is also more likely to occur in people of African (open angle) or Asian (angle closure) origin. Once detected, glaucoma can be treated with eye drops and possibly surgery. See chapter 4 for more details.

Diabetic eye disease occurs due to diabetic damage to the blood vessels in the retina at the back of the eye. It is more likely to occur if you have had diabetes for a number of years, and is most likely to occur if your diabetes is poorly managed. Damage can occur without you being aware of it, or you may have blurred patches of vision. You can find your vision changes from day to day. Once detected, diabetic eye disease can be treated in a number of ways. See chapter 6 for more details.

A cataract occurs when the lens inside your eye becomes cloudy. It can make your vision blurred and yellowed. You can find bright lights dazzling and have problems with glare on a sunny day or from car headlights. The cloudiness in the lens grows gradually over time. Cataracts can be removed and the lens replaced to improve your vision. See chapter 5 for more details.

A detached retina can cause a shadow at the edge of your vision or create an effect like a curtain falling over a large part of your sight in one eye. It is more common in people who have moderate to severe short sight because the retina may be thinner than average. You may experience flashes of light or a dramatic increase in 'floaters', black dots in front of the eyes, in the run up to a retinal detachment. The condition is not painful, but if you have symptoms like this you should see an ophthalmologist straightaway.

More causes of sight loss

- Some people have sight problems from birth. Some are caused by the mother having an infection while the baby is in the womb. This could be an infection like rubella, also known as German measles, or toxocara which comes from animal faeces. Premature birth can also lead to sight problems.

- Some eye conditions like retinitis pigmentosa are inherited and get worse over time. People with albinism (lack of eye pigment) or nystagmus (shaky eyes) also have reduced vision from birth, which rarely changes with age.

- The most common cause of sight loss in younger adults is injury to one eye. Health problems like stroke can also cause sudden loss of sight.

- Optometrist Nick Rumney adds, 'Approximately 1 in 10 people have reduced vision due to poor development of vision. This is commonly referred to as a lazy eye, but the technical term is amblyopia.'

Looking after your eyes

Whether you know you have sight problems or you just want to look after your eyes, there are things you can do to help your eyes stay healthy.

Stop smoking

According to RNIB, smoking is the number one threat to the health of your eyes. It can cause macular degeneration and cataracts, two of the leading causes of sight loss. Smoking can reduce the blood flow at the back of the eye, causing damage to the macula, the part of the eye that is essential for detailed vision. Tobacco smoke contains heavy metals which accumulate in the lens at the front of the eye, leading to a cataract.

Passive smoking can cause almost as many problems. Like smokers, people who have been exposed to other's smoke over five years almost double their chances of macular degeneration.

'Whether you know you have sight problems or you just want to look after your eyes, there are things you can do to help your eyes stay healthy.'

So, if you are a smoker and want to protect your eyes, the first thing to do is to stop smoking. If you stop, the increased risk of eye disease will reverse over time. Talk to your GP or pop into a pharmacy to find out about stopping smoking with the support of a professional.

Eat well

Poor nutrition can contribute to sight problems, particularly macular degeneration. Vitamins and minerals, known as antioxidants, help protect the back of the eye from chemicals called 'free radicals' in our bloodstream.

'Vitamins and minerals, known as antioxidants, help protect the back of the eye from chemicals called "free radicals" in our bloodstream.'

Two antioxidants, lutein and zeaxanthin (pronounced zee-uh-zan'-thin) are thought by some experts to prevent damage to the macula by free radicals. They may be able to prevent macular degeneration developing, and two studies have shown lutein to improve vision. It is not yet certain that supplements containing lutein and zeaxanthin will provide benefits when you have a balanced diet, but studies are taking place to investigate this. A study is also looking at the possible benefits of omega 3 fatty acids, which are found in fish, cutting the risk of developing macular degeneration or slowing its progression.

Research suggests that a diet high in polyunsaturated fats, and particularly the consumption of fish that is rich in these fats, decreases the risk of developing macular degeneration and may slow down the progression of this condition from moderate to severe. Vitamins A, C and E as part of a healthy diet may have a role in protecting against cataracts.

Don't start taking lots of supplements: instead, make sure your diet is packed with healthy foods. Try to consume foods from the groups listed in the table shown opposite.

Sources of vitamins A, C and E	Sources of lutein	Sources of zeaxanthin
Oranges	Yellow peppers	Orange sweet peppers
Kiwis	Mango	Broccoli
Grapefruit	Bilberries/blueberries	Corn
Dried apricots	Green leafy vegetables	Lettuce (not iceberg)
Green leafy vegetables		Spinach
Tomatoes		Tangerines
Peppers		Oranges
Raw carrots		Eggs
Green peas		
Green beans		
Brussels sprouts		
Nuts		
Seeds		
Dairy produce		
Eggs		

In addition, eat omega-3 rich oily fish twice a week for women and girls who might one day have a baby, and four times a week for men and boys. If you then feel you need to take supplements talk to your GP. The supplements on sale in pharmacies and supermarkets can have a useful role if you can't manage to eat your five a day or oily fish.

Wear sunglasses

Excess exposure to UV light plays a part in both macular degeneration and cataract development. Wearing UV absorbing sunglasses or a broad brimmed hat reduces your sunlight exposure and may help reduce the risk of some sorts of cataract and possibly macular degeneration too. Choose sunglasses with the CE marking, as this shows that they meet European safety standards.

Nick Rumney explains, 'Sunglasses without this mark may not have UV absorbance and are dangerous to use as they may actually let more UV into the eye.'

'Wearing UV absorbing sunglasses or a broad brimmed hat reduces your sunlight exposure and may help reduce the risk of some sorts of cataract and possibly macular degeneration too.'

Manage your diabetes

If you have diabetes, try to manage it as well as possible. Diabetic eye disease is more likely to occur earlier and is likely to be more severe if your control is poor. Speak to your specialist if you have problems with controlling your diabetes. You should be invited to have your eyes checked every year: make sure you attend as it is easier to treat diabetic eye problems if they are detected early on.

A number of people may not be aware that they have diabetes, and could be developing eye disease without realising. If you feel excessively tired without cause, need to urinate frequently and are often thirsty, ask your GP for advice. Get more advice on the symptoms of diabetes from the Diabetes UK website at www.diabetes.org.uk.

Watch your weight

If you are overweight, you can have a high risk of eye problems. Obesity is linked to high blood pressure, high cholesterol, diabetes and heart disease. It has also been recently linked to all the leading causes of sight loss, macular degeneration, diabetic eye disease, cataract and possibly glaucoma too. High blood pressure can damage the blood vessels in the retina at the back of the eye. High cholesterol can cause the arteries in the retina to harden and thicken, pressing on and blocking veins. This can cause fluid leaks at the back of the eye and sight damage. If you are overweight or obese, ask your GP for advice on healthy and sustainable weight loss.

Get your eyes tested

Not all sight loss can be controlled. However healthy you are, there are other factors at play, for example, glaucoma runs in families. What's more, many eye diseases don't have symptoms in the early stages, so you may not be able to tell that your sight is being damaged. Regular eye tests can help pick up the very early signs of disease. The optometrist looks at the back of the eye to spot conditions like macular degeneration, diabetic eye disease and can even see signs of high blood pressure. Get your eyes tested every two years, or more often if advised. People with a family history of glaucoma may need an annual test.

How you feel about sight loss

If you have recently found out that your sight is getting worse, you will be going through a range of emotions. Different people experience these feelings to a varying extent, but you may be going through some of the following:

- Denial – most people go through a period of denial, as this can help you get through the difficult initial phase.

- Anger – it is normal to feel anger. You may be asking 'Why Me?'

- Grief, sadness and loss – at times you will feel a devastating sense of grief and loss for the things you are unable to do right now.

- Acknowledgement – it can take time, but eventually you will move into a phase where you can acknowledge what is happening to you.

- Coping well – at some point you will find that living with sight loss is now the norm for you and you are coping well again.

Getting support

It isn't easy to go through these emotions; you may feel all at sea in a world that is suddenly unfriendly. Your usual sources of information, leaflets or the Internet may be hard to access. People who haven't experienced sight loss may not appear to understand what you are going through, and you may find it harder to get out and see friends, leaving you even more isolated. Nick Rumney suggests, 'Mostly the hardest part is knowing the questions to ask.'

Don't despair: there are services to help. Start by calling RNIB's helpline (see help list). RNIB also offers an emotional support telephone service run by a team of telephone counsellors. Talking to a counsellor gives you the chance to share how you feel without worrying about burdening a friend or relative. A counsellor can:

- Give you time to talk about your situation.

- Listen to how you are feeling.

- Help you to identify what you need.

- Help you work out the best way to get it.

Through the RNIB helpline or emotional support telephone service, you can be put in touch with support in your local area through befriending, or support groups. Everything you share with the trained counsellors is confidential.

If you have macular degeneration, the Macular Disease Society also offers counselling (see help list).

If you have been diagnosed with eye disease at hospital, they may have a trained worker to help talk you through what you are experiencing. Ask if there is a patient support service or an eye clinic liaison officer who can:

- Provide you with emotional support and help you come to terms with your eye condition.
- Give you information about your eye condition in an accessible format.
- Explain what you can expect to happen next.
- Put you in touch with your local sensory impairment/rehabilitation social care teams.
- Tell you about the help and benefits you might be able to get.
- Talk to you about registering your visual impairment.

RNIB also run 'finding your feet' weekends for people new to sight loss. These are three day events, held in hotels around the UK. Together with others in similar situations, you can talk through how you feel and learn about practical solutions to the challenges of living with blindness or partial sight.

Which professionals will you meet?

- Optometrist – working in a slightly different role in the low vision clinic, the optometrist assesses remaining vision and helps you access different strategies to improve vision, e.g. low vision aids (magnifiers) or lighting. Sometimes this service is delivered by a dispensing optician.
- Rehabilitation officer – a rehabilitation officer can help you learn new ways of doing things and help you cope emotionally too. They will talk through what you need and come up with a plan to meet those needs.

A rehabilitation officer can:

- Offer emotional support and financial advice.
- Teach you how to get around safely at home and outdoors.
- Work with you on getting to the places you usually visit.
- Teach you new ways to do things at home.
- Show you useful aids and equipment.
- Help with specialist issues such as employment or parenting.
- Refer you on for further help if needed.

Advice for carers

Losing your sight is a challenging life experience. If you live with or care for someone experiencing serious sight problems, they will be going through a range of emotions. People may seem to be coping well at one moment, and not the next. You can help them by:

- Listening – you don't always need to be able to provide a solution, sometimes just sharing how they feel can make the person feel better.

- Supporting the person to get out and continue their usual activities – it is easy to become isolated when your sight deteriorates, which can lead to depression and lower quality of life.

Quick action checklist

Now you've read this chapter, ask yourself do you need to:

- Book an eye test?
- Talk to your GP about your diet?
- Call the RNIB helpline?
- Contact the eye clinic to find out about support available locally?

Summing Up

- Sight loss is something that happens to many people as they get older. There are some common causes of sight loss, most of which can be treated. If you are concerned about your sight, make sure you speak to an eye care professional. Look after your eyes by stopping smoking and eating a healthy diet rich in fresh fruit and vegetables.

- If you are going through sight loss, it can be a difficult time. Call the RNIB helpline or ask at your eye clinic for sources of support.

Chapter Three

Macular Degeneration

Macular degeneration is the leading cause of sight loss in the UK. In this chapter you can find out:

- What the macula is and why it is critical for sight.
- The changes that happen with age and whether there is anything you can do to protect your macula.
- The treatment and help available if you are experiencing macular degeneration.

What is the macula?

The back of your eye is covered with cells that detect light. These cells form part of the layer known as the retina. The macula is at the centre of the retina and is densely packed with cells that allow you to see fine details in colour.

'The macula is responsible for fine vision, such as reading and recognising people.'

Som Prasad, ophthalmologist.

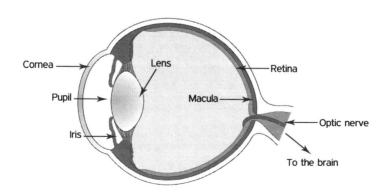

About macular degeneration

In macular degeneration there is damage to the cells in the macula. In the early stages this can cause small print to appear unclear or distorted. As one eye is usually affected before the other, you may not notice these early changes. There is no pain with the condition. As it progresses, the central distortion or fuzziness can turn into a blank spot which makes it hard to read small print or recognise faces. Macular degeneration does not usually lead to total sight loss: if you have the condition, you are likely to retain your side vision, enabling you to get around a bit easier than without.

Before   *After*

© Som Prasad.

Wet macular degeneration

Wet macular degeneration happens when new blood vessels grow behind the macula. Blood leakages and scarring prevent the cells from working well and central vision becomes poor. This type of macular degeneration is less common, accounting for around 1 case in 10, but left untreated it leads to more severe visual loss. Happily, there are now treatments that can stabilise the condition, but they are not a cure.

Dry macular degeneration

Dry macular degeneration happens when debris builds up behind the macula. The cells of the macula become unhealthy, so the signals which would allow you to see are no longer carried by nerves from the back of the eye to the brain.

It is the more common form of the condition and tends to happen to older people. Ophthalmologist Som Prasad explains, 'it is usually gradually progressive and may lead to moderate visual loss. However, this is often not severe. Effective treatments are not yet available.'

There are strategies to help you cope better despite the damage. People with macular degeneration will usually find properly prescribed magnifiers helpful, although in its early stages simple over-the-counter magnifiers will be a good start.

Macular degeneration is also known as age-related macular degeneration (you may find this abbreviated as AMD) as it usually occurs in older people. Younger people can experience sight loss due to problems with the macula. These problems are generally known as macular dystrophies, which can run in families.

What causes macular degeneration?

We don't know exactly why macular degeneration takes place.

- The condition is more common in older people. There can be signs of macular degeneration in 1 in 10 people aged 66 to 74 and around 1 in 3 people aged 75 to 85.

- Women are more likely to have macular degeneration than men.

- Family history – some sorts of macular degeneration seem to run in families.

- Smoking is linked to macular degeneration.

- In some, but not all, research papers it has been suggested that increased exposure to the sun over a lifetime may increase the risk of macular degeneration.

- Macular degeneration is more likely to be found in Caucasians than in people of African descent.

- High blood pressure can increase the risk.

- Protecting your eyes from the sun, eating a well-balanced diet with plenty of fresh fruits and vegetables and stopping smoking may all help to delay the progress of macular degeneration.

Recent research has looked at how certain supplements can cut the chance of developing macular degeneration or slow down its progress. One study showed that supplements including vitamin C and vitamin E, which are known as antioxidants, helped when taken in combination with zinc. Lutein and zeaxanthin, found in green leafy vegetables and eggs have also been shown to have protective effects. More trials are going on to test the effect of these in combination with fish oils. However, ophthalmologist Som Prasad advises, 'These are not indicated for everyone and there are health risks from taking very high levels of certain supplements, especially if you are a smoker or have been in the last 10 years, so it is important to consult your doctor before taking these supplements.'

See chapter 2 for more about foods that contribute to good eye health. You can buy two recipe books with relevant recipes written by an ophthalmologist from the Macular Disease Society (see help list).

Detecting macular degeneration

You may notice changes in your central vision yourself. Book an appointment with an optometrist for an eye test and ask them to check the back of the eye for signs of macular degeneration.

Sometimes the condition can be picked up as part of your routine eye test and you may be unaware of problems yourself. Optometrist Nick Rumney explains, 'Some optometrists have started to use new instruments that scan the retina for changes in structure. These instruments will show the earliest signs of retinal change, but you may have to pay extra for this test as it is not covered by the NHS.'

If you are concerned about the condition or the optometrist sees changes at the back of the eye, they may check your eyes with an Amsler grid. This is a chart with a grid pattern on it. The practitioner will ask you to cover one eye and look at the chart. In early macular degeneration, the central part of your vision is distorted. Later on in the disease, the central area of a grid would be missing altogether.

If you want to monitor your own central visual field, it can help you detect early visual changes.

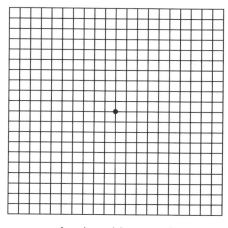 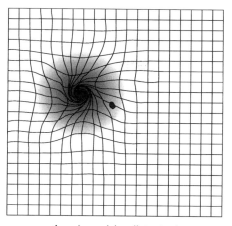

Amsler grid - normal   *Amsler grid - distorted*

- Cover one eye, so you can spot changes in each eye in turn.
- Make sure you have good lighting on the page.
- Wear your usual reading glasses, if you need them.
- Cover your right eye (without pressing hard).
- Use your left eye to stare at the spot in the centre of the grid.
- Keep your eye still, and notice the horizontal and vertical lines to the left and right, above and below the central dot. Are any of them blurry, distorted, missing or wiggly?
- Then repeat the test with your other eye covered.

If you notice any problems, repeat the test after a few hours. If the lines remain distorted or broken, make an appointment with your optometrist.

Find a video on how to test yourself with an Amsler grid and a copy to print and download at http://sight2020.co.uk/amsler.aspx.

If your GP or optometrist detects signs of macular degeneration, they will refer you to an ophthalmologist at a hospital. Nick Rumney advises, 'The referral may be urgent (so-called fast track) in the case of wet AMD or routine (for untreatable dry AMD).'

You will be sent an appointment to see the ophthalmologist. You will be given eye drops which widen your pupils to give the specialist a clearer view inside. These drops can leave your vision blurry for a few hours, so take someone with you to drive home.

The ophthalmologist will use a bright light to look inside your eye. In some cases, that will enable them to diagnose macular degeneration. Alternatively, they may use a new sort of computerised scanner (called OCT) which can see the layers beneath the retina. They should explain about the progression of the disease and talk about the sort of help you can get.

'The ophthalmologist will use a bright light to look inside your eye. In some cases, that will enable them to diagnose macular degeneration.'

If the specialist needs further information about changes at the back of the eye, they may suggest that you have a test that uses a dye injected into a vein in your arm to show up the path of the blood vessels around your macula. This test is called fluorescein angiography, often termed FFA. Dye is injected into your arm and travels to the blood vessels at the back of the eye. The specialist then takes photographs using blue light (you may feel dazzled or nauseous during and after the test, but it is not painful). The test helps the ophthalmologist understand what sort of macular degeneration is present and whether treatment can help.

Treatment

There are now well-established treatments for the wet form of macular degeneration, while other newer treatments are being evaluated.

NICE is the government body that looks at treatments and decides which should be available on the NHS. It has looked at various treatments for macular degeneration. Ophthalmologist Som Prasad explains, 'NICE recommends that for most patients with wet AMD treatment, Lucentis (ranibizumab) is effective and should be available to patients fitting defined treatment criteria in the NHS.' NICE will also assess new treatments as they become available. If you have access to the Internet, you can download NICE assessments (for wet AMD look at http://guidance.nice.org.uk/TA155 and for moderately advanced dry AMD look at http://guidance.nice.org.uk/IPG272/Guidance/pdf/English). This will give you some knowledge to help you discuss possible treatments with your ophthalmologist.

Treatment for wet macular degeneration

There are lots of ongoing developments in the area of treatment for wet macular degeneration. Most treatments cannot bring back damaged cells, but can stop your vision getting worse. Treatments that may offer some visual improvement for some people are available.

The sight problems with wet macular degeneration are due to blood vessels growing where they affect the cells you use for detailed vision. Treatment needs to happen as soon as possible because your vision can get worse quickly with wet macular degeneration.

Drug treatments (known as anti-angiogenics or anti-vascular endothelial growth factor agents) work by reducing the growth of blood vessels, cutting bleeding and leaking. The drug is injected into the gel inside your eye and can stop blood vessels growing and even cause them to regress, which might improve your sight. The injection is painless and needs to be repeated every month for the first three months then on an 'as required' basis. Monthly follow-ups with your ophthalmic team are required in the long term to enable early intervention and re-intervention when needed. This treatment is usually only suitable for people with recent onset of wet macular degeneration. Som Prasad explains, 'Unfortunately, people with long standing visual loss due to wet AMD usually have scar formation in the macula already and do not benefit from these treatments.'

'No one has yet found a successful treatment for dry macular degeneration. At present, there are research projects looking at stem cell and gene therapy.'

Treatment for dry macular degeneration

No one has yet found a successful treatment for dry macular degeneration. At present, there are research projects looking at stem cell and gene therapy. You can get news of research projects on the Macular Disease Society website (see help list).

Although there is no treatment for the condition, this does not mean that nothing can be done to help you. You can use your remaining vision with the assistance of magnifiers, equipment, training and support – see chapters 7 and 8. Nick Rumney advises, 'Over three quarters of all people with low vision can be helped with simple magnifiers and advice on appropriate lighting. However, even a simple magnifier needs careful use and you may need to be shown how to use it. Be sure to ask about having a low vision assessment.'

To find out about equipment that might help, you can contact RNIB, or speak to your GP or local authority's social care department about local support. The Macular Disease Society has a leaflet about low vision aids and also offers a counselling service. There is likely to be a group for people with sight problems local to you that can help you with practical training and support – just contact the Macular Disease Society.

Case study

'When my dad's sight began to fail as a result of macular degeneration, I had my first experience of what life is like for people with sight loss. The world isn't designed for people with poor sight – at the local supermarket, for example, labels are written in such small print that they're almost impossible to read if you have less than perfect sight.

'Help can be hard to come by. When my dad went to the council offices to ask if he could apply for council accommodation, he was given a form to fill in. He explained that, because of his sight, he couldn't read the form or fill it in properly, and asked the council employee to help. She refused, telling him she wasn't allowed to fill it in and he would have to ask a friend to do it. At 84, he has several health problems, but when he asked his GP surgery to print their letters to him in a bigger typeface, they refused.

'He has been lucky in some respects. Social services have been good at providing him with simple adaptive technology and letting him know what's available. Because he's in Wales, the Welsh Assembly's Low Vision Scheme entitles him to a free hand-held electronic magnifier that would normally cost £295. That will be invaluable when it comes to those supermarket shops.

'Nonetheless, it isn't easy for him because he lives alone. Life would be easier for him, and for many others in similar positions, if those in authority were willing to be a little more flexible in their dealings with people with low vision – and there are an awful lot of them about.' Kim.

Advice for carers

Macular degeneration can be frustrating for the person experiencing it. Suddenly it can become harder to read small print, look up telephone numbers, tell the time on your watch and more. It is also confusing because your peripheral vision may be unaffected.

- Make things easier by ensuring that there is good light at home. Look into obtaining large print or talking books and write notes in a clear, bold pen.

- Support the person you care for to find out more about local low vision services so they can access magnifiers and other equipment to help them keep some independence.

- If your loved one lacks confidence getting out and about, check the Macular Disease Society's information on being a 'sighted guide' for someone with sight problems.

- You can also enquire about the availability of mobility training through the local rehabilitation officer. Local branches of the Macular Disease Society often offer excellent support and are well worth getting in touch with.

Quick action checklist

- If you think you might have macular problems, make an appointment for an eye test: the first stop is usually your own optician. If one eye is already affected and you are getting symptoms in the other eye, most NHS or private retinal specialists will have a rapid access system in place which you can access directly or through your GP.

- If you have been diagnosed with macular degeneration and are having problems, ask your GP about getting help and support with everyday living. You can also find out about your local low vision service through your local social care department, the Macular Disease Society and RNIB.

Summing Up

- Macular degeneration affects your central vision. It can cause serious sight loss, but will almost always leave your side vision unaffected, allowing you to get out and about.

- There are effective treatment options for people with recent onset wet macular degeneration.

- People with advanced conditions, which are untreatable, find magnifiers and other technology helpful to enable them to lead a productive and enjoyable life.

- There are support groups locally and nationally where you can get advice and share your experiences.

Chapter Four

Glaucoma

Glaucoma affects more than 500,000 people in England and Wales alone. It principally affects those aged 40 and over: 2% of people aged 40 or over have glaucoma and this rises to almost 10% of those over 75.

Glaucoma is almost always painless, which means that unless you have regular eye checks with an optometrist, it can damage your eyesight without you realising. It is the leading cause of preventable blindness in the UK.

Glaucoma can run in families: if you have a close relative with the condition, you have four times the chance of developing it. People of African or African-Caribbean origin have about four times the risk of primary open angle glaucoma (POAG) compared to Caucasians. People of Asian descent have a greatly increased incidence of angle closure glaucoma (see overleaf).

People aged 40 and over with a close relative with glaucoma are entitled to a free NHS eye examination. However, if repeat tests of pressure or field are needed, in some situations the cost of these extra tests is not paid for by the NHS.

If you have been told that you have glaucoma, you will need monitoring and treatment for the rest of your life to help protect your sight.

What is glaucoma?

Everyone's eyes are filled with fluid, known as 'aqueous humour'. This aqueous fluid helps keep your eyeball in shape and circulates through a tiny meshwork around the edge of your iris.

'Glaucoma is almost always painless, which means that unless you have regular eye checks with an optometrist, it can damage your eyesight without you realising.'

In some people, the pressure of the fluid is raised and damages the optic nerve, which carries messages from your eye to your brain. In other people, although the pressure is not raised, there may be a weakness which causes similar nerve damage. In many people, it can be a combination of nerve weakness and raised pressure which predisposes them to glaucoma.

The damage to the optic nerve usually takes place gradually. A small patch of vision is affected first. Most people won't spot this initially as the other eye makes up for the loss.

If left untreated your sight would slowly decrease from the edge inwards, so you miss things at the periphery of your vision. This causes problems with getting about as you won't see hazards coming in from the side.

Over time, untreated glaucoma causes tunnel vision, where you can only see things straight ahead. In severe cases, this can make it hard to read as you are unable to scan pages and can only focus on a small area of print at a time.

Types of glaucoma

Primary open angle glaucoma

Most of the time when we talk about glaucoma, we mean primary open angle glaucoma (POAG). This is painless and in the early stage you will have no warning signs.

In POAG, the fluid in the eye can flow to the meshwork, but its flow is then restricted. The blockage happens slowly over many years, and the pressure in your eye increases gradually too.

What is 'normal' pressure?

NICE has issued guidance that people with eye pressure of over 21mmHg should be referred for further investigation. This is the case if the raised pressure is in one or both eyes.

Further guidance for optometrists has been published by the College of Optometrists and Royal College of Ophthalmologists which advises that certain people, who are at a very low risk and have no other signs of glaucoma, may not need referral as above. For example, if you are aged 65 and over, you should be referred if your pressure is 25mmHg and over, or 26mmHg and over if you are aged 80 plus.

Diagnosing glaucoma is often not cut and dried and this may mean that several visits might be needed before a clear decision is made. It is important to realise that there is no one single sign that diagnoses glaucoma, and a decision is only reached after reviewing the assessment or reassessment of different risk factors.

If you have raised pressure and no signs of damage to the nerves in the eye, this is called 'ocular hypertension'. This could affect between 3-5% of people aged over 40, and means that you may be at risk of this converting to glaucoma in the future. Many people simply require monitoring without treatment. You will be asked to come back for regular checks and may be offered eye drops to protect your sight if the risk of conversion is considered too high.

A smaller number of people have a type of POAG where the pressure is within normal levels. This is known as normal tension glaucoma. It may be due to poor blood circulation around the optic nerve. As with other types of glaucoma, treatment aims to lower the pressure in your eye to a level where the nerves do not suffer further damage.

Angle closure glaucoma

An uncommon type of glaucoma is angle closure glaucoma. This happens when the circulation of fluid round the eye is blocked slowly or suddenly. It can be caused by a narrow opening or 'angle' between the front of the iris and the drainage meshwork in the eye. It is often sudden and painful and can cause permanent damage if untreated. If you experience a sudden, painful eye, you should call NHS Direct (0845 46 47) for advice straightaway.

Other types of glaucoma

■ Glaucoma can sometimes be caused by other eye problems. This is known as secondary glaucoma.

■ A very small number of babies are born with a problem that causes the pressure to rise in their eyes. This is known as congenital glaucoma.

Who is at risk of glaucoma?

For POAG, the most common type of glaucoma in the UK, there are several well-known risk factors. You have a higher risk of the condition if:

■ You are over 40 – the risk increases as you age, so glaucoma is present in 5% of people over 65.

■ You are of African or African-Caribbean descent – the condition can develop at an earlier age and be more severe.

■ You have a close blood relative who has glaucoma – you should get your eyes checked every year once you are aged over 40: you are entitled to a free NHS eye test.

■ You are very short sighted.

■ You have diabetes, as this is believed to increase your risk of glaucoma.

For angle closure glaucoma, the risk is higher in women than men, and it occurs more in people of East Asian or Inuit descent.

How is glaucoma detected?

We've already noted that you won't be able to feel or spot the early changes caused by POAG, so how can it be detected? Fortunately, these early changes can be spotted as part of a routine eye examination.

Everyone should get their eyes checked at least every two years, and more often if your optician advises. If you have a close family member with glaucoma, the International Glaucoma Association recommends that you are tested for glaucoma from the age of 35 onwards. If you are at higher risk of POAG because you are African-Caribbean, or angle closure glaucoma because you are Asian, or if you have diabetes, mention this every time you have an eye test and ask to be checked for glaucoma, whatever your age.

During the eye test the optometrist will carry out some tests to help them get a picture of your overall eye health. They will:

- Look at the back of your eye with a light – in glaucoma, the 'optic nerve head' (where the optic nerve leaves the eye) changes its appearance, which can be picked up with this test.

- Measure the pressure in your eye – this can be done using an instrument that blows a puff of air on the eye or using blue light and a small probe that rests gently on the surface of your eye.

- Check your field of vision. You will be asked to put your chin on a rest and look at a screen where small spots of light will flash up one after another.

Despite the fact that these tests are straightforward, painless and can be done at most high street opticians, according to the International Glaucoma Association, research has shown that more than half of all cases of POAG remain undetected. Optometrist Nick Rumney advises, 'It can take 2-5 years for a first suspicion of glaucoma to become definite enough to require referral. Unfortunately, pressure tests are very poor detectors of glaucoma on their own. At least half of all glaucoma diagnosis occurs within normal pressure ranges. The pressure test is certainly not a glaucoma test. Because the changes over time are subtle, you should not shop around amongst opticians because the continuity of the records is very important.'

If your eye pressure is raised, your optometrist may invite you back for a further check to see if this is always the case. Optometrists are not paid to do secondary testing and may charge you for this.

If the optometrist spots signs of glaucoma, they will write a letter explaining this to your GP. Your GP will then pass these details on to the hospital eye department. You will then be sent an appointment to see an ophthalmologist.

At the hospital you will have tests that are similar to those at the opticians, plus further assessments. NICE recommends that to diagnose glaucoma, the ophthalmologist should:

- Check the pressure in your eye using 'Goldmann applanation tonometry', where you put your chin on a rest, a blue light is shone on the eye and a small probe is rested gently on the eye surface. The ophthalmologist will use eye drops with this test. If you normally wear contact lenses, bring your glasses with you to the appointment as you will be advised not to put the lenses back in.

- Examine your eye with a special device that touches the surface of your eye gently to measure the thickness of the cornea (the clear front part of your eye).

- Assess the depth of the angle between the front of your iris and the back of your cornea, leading to the meshwork that the aqueous fluid should pass through.

- Check your field of vision. You will be asked to put your chin on a rest and look at a screen where small spots of light will flash up one after another. This can be a hard test to do and you may need to repeat it several times to get a good result.

- Use eye drops to get a clear view of the back of the eye to see if the head of the optic nerve is showing any signs of change due to glaucoma. The drops used in this test can leave your vision blurred for a short while after the test, so you shouldn't drive yourself home afterwards.

Treatment

After these tests, the ophthalmologist should be able to make a diagnosis. Glaucoma can be treated with various different drugs – mainly eye drops – that can help you keep the vision you have left. However, if your sight has been damaged already, there is not yet a treatment that can regain lost vision – treatment can only protect the vision that you have. The International Glaucoma Association estimate that around 95% of those diagnosed early with glaucoma in the UK will retain useful sight for life.

The main treatments for glaucoma are eye drops, laser treatment and drainage surgery.

Eye drops

Eye drops help your eyes by opening up the drainage meshwork in your eye or reducing the amount of fluid produced to reduce the pressure in your eye.

Laser treatment

If eye drops alone do not reduce the pressure enough to prevent continuing visual field loss, you may also be offered laser treatment. This treatment is usually for angle closure glaucoma only.

Drainage surgery

Drainage surgery, also known as 'trabeculectomy', creates a channel that the fluid in the eye can drain out through. You may need to use eye drops too after surgery.

At the appointment you should have the chance to talk about your diagnosis, and ask about what might happen in the future. You should remember that:

- Glaucoma is usually symptomless and you'll need to have regular check-ups in order to monitor it.
- You must persist with the treatment in order to protect your remaining sight.

Your specialist should give you relevant information in a format that you can read, and hospital eye clinics should also have audio information available.

After your initial appointment, if you are prescribed eye drops you will be invited back within a few months to check that the drops are having the necessary effect.

If everything progresses well, you will continue to use your eye drops and have check-ups at regular intervals, every six months or annually depending on what your consultant advises.

If you are confused by any of the terms used during your appointment or want to find out more, the International Glaucoma Association has an excellent glossary on their website and can also answer questions through their helpline (see help list).

'Your specialist should give you relevant information in a format that you can read, and hospital eye clinics should also have audio information available.'

For videos about glaucoma from ophthalmologist Som Prasad, see http:// sight2020.co.uk/glaucoma.aspx.

Glaucoma in the long term

If you are given eye drops, you will need to continue to use these for life unless your ophthalmologist changes your treatment or suggests laser treatment or surgery.

Once you have glaucoma, you will get your eyes checked at the hospital on a regular basis. Your ophthalmologist will let you know if the damage to your eyes is enough to cause problems with driving, and the International Glaucoma Association offers a useful leaflet about driving when you have glaucoma.

If you already have sight loss due to glaucoma, there are a number of ways to help you make the most of the vision that you do have. At your hospital appointment, ask to speak to a low vision specialist or rehabilitation officer. They can advise you on available aids and gadgets to help with day-to-day living (see chapters 7 and 8 for more information).

'At your hospital appointment, ask to speak to a low vision specialist or rehabilitation officer. They can advise you on available aids and gadgets to help with day-to-day living.'

Advice for carers

- If you are a blood relative of someone with glaucoma, make sure that you are checked for the condition yourself. Pass this message on to other family members, especially those nearing their 40s.

- If you care for someone with sight loss due to glaucoma, be aware that mobility and moving around is where they are most likely to experience problems. When crossing the road, they will need to make a point of turning their head and using their hearing to double-check for cars.

- Inserting eye drops can cause problems for older people and anyone with arthritic fingers. There are various eye drop dispensers available to make the process of inserting eye drops much easier. These are available through the RNIB shop (see help list).

Quick action checklist

▨ If you have been diagnosed with glaucoma, tell your blood relatives to get their eyes checked for glaucoma. This is important for those nearing their 40s and above.

▨ If you're in need of help and support, visit the International Glaucoma Association's website or call their helpline (see help list).

Summing Up

- Glaucoma covers a range of conditions, but the most common type of glaucoma causes slow and painless sight loss. Eye tests are vital to detect the condition.

- If you've been told that you have glaucoma, the good news is that treatment can begin immediately to help to preserve your sight. You may be offered eye drops, laser treatment or surgery. If you are told to use eye drops, continue to use these every day unless your consultant tells you otherwise.

- If you have sight problems due to glaucoma, there are practical things you can do to make day-to-day life easier. See chapters 7 and 8 for more information on this.

Chapter Five

Cataracts

More than half of people aged 65 and older have some signs of cataracts and it is present for almost everyone over 75. If you have been told that you have a cataract, the good news is that this is a treatable cause of sight loss.

What is a cataract?

Inside your eye is a clear lens which focuses rays of light on the back of the eye. As you get older the lens can become less clear, which is known as a cataract. It causes problems because the clouding of the lens cuts the amount of light that passes through and scatters the light that does get through, thus dimming and blurring the vision.

For older people, cataracts develop slowly and painlessly and as yet there is no way to prevent them. Although there are supplements on the market which claim to help slow the progression of eye problems, including cataracts, medical opinion is divided on whether these help and there is no robust evidence for their benefits. Professionals suggest eating a balanced diet with plenty of fruit and vegetables, particularly green leafy vegetables.

Causes of cataracts

The majority of cataracts are due to old age. However, they can occur due to other reasons including:

- Injury.
- Certain types of medication.
- Illnesses such as diabetes.

- Longstanding inflammation.
- A tiny number of babies are born with cataracts.
- Some research papers show that smoking, poor diet and exposure to sunlight may accelerate cataract development.

Detection

You might start to notice changes in your vision, for example:

- Your vision is less clear than before, things might seem blurry – a bit like looking through slightly frosted glass.
- Some people notice a colour change, particularly if a cataract is present in one eye only For example, when your vision might develop a yellowish tint.
- You might find that vision in one eye is more blurred than in the other.
- You might have problems with night vision and find that lights, such as oncoming headlights, cause glare. Equally, bright sunny days can cause problems for the same reason.

If you have noticed anything like this happening to you, make an appointment for an eye test.

Treatment

Initially, you may find that an update to your spectacle prescription improves your vision, but as the cataract continues to develop you will need further help. When you find that your vision is causing problems with your life, ask your optometrist to write a note to your GP explaining that you have a cataract. Some optometrists can refer you directly to an eye specialist and simply notify your GP that they have done so.

Nick Rumney explains, 'Optometrists will refer when the following three things occur: a cataract causes visual loss; the cataract is having an impact on your quality of life (e.g. problems with driving); and you are ready, willing and able to undertake surgery.'

'Initially, you may find that an update to your spectacle prescription improves your vision, but as the cataract continues to develop you will need further help.'

Delaying your referral will not reduce the likelihood of a good outcome from surgery so you can take some time to think it over and do it when it's right for you. Your GP will arrange for you to be seen at the hospital eye clinic to discuss if an operation to remove the cataract is appropriate. At this appointment the eye specialist will look at your eyes and ask you in detail about any visual problems that you are having. They will also ask about your general health to ensure that the operation is suitable for you. Before agreeing to surgery they will outline the risks and benefits of the operation and make sure that you understand what will happen. Your eyes will be measured to work out the correct strength of replacement lens that would suit you best. Surgeons will generally operate on one eye at a time in case there are any problems.

Nick Rumney advises, 'Remember, modern medicine will never tell you what you should do, the final decision is always yours. As a general rule you will not be offered the possibility of surgery unless the surgeon is sure that you would benefit.'

Currently, the majority of cataract operations are performed as day surgery under a local anaesthetic. You won't need to stay overnight in hospital, but you must make sure you arrange for someone else to take you home.

Before the operation, your surgeon may discuss whether to reduce your main spectacle prescription by selecting an implant to make you independent of spectacles for most tasks other than reading. Optometrist Nick Rumney advises, 'If you were short sighted before surgery and have been used to reading without glasses and only using glasses for distance, you may wish to stay this way. Spend some time making sure you are really clear about the outcome the surgeon intends you to have.'

During the operation

When you have cataract surgery, you will be given an anaesthetic so that you don't feel what is happening. For most people this is a local anaesthetic consisting of an injection or sometimes just eye drops alone. You will be awake, but the anaesthetist will make sure you do not feel the area around your eye. You will hear the eye specialist explaining what they are doing, but you will not see anything that is going on. At most, you will be aware of some vague movements around the eye.

Brian Little is a consultant specialising in cataracts at Moorfields Eye Hospital. He explains, 'You do not have to worry about keeping your eye open as this will be controlled by the surgeon without you being aware of it.'

The specialist makes a tiny incision in the eye to remove the cataract and will, in most cases, insert a plastic replacement lens to continue the job of focusing light on the back of your eye. Brian Little explains, 'This will usually take around 30 minutes. Your eye may then be covered to help protect it for the next 24 hours, as it starts to recover.'

After the operation

'There are now lens implants available that are "multifocal" and these enable you to see for distance and for reading without the need for glasses.'

Brian Little, ophthalmologist.

You will be told how to look after your eye before you leave the hospital. You will also be given eye drops to use for the next month to prevent infection and inflammation. Brian Little explains, 'Your eye will look a little red and feel somewhat gritty in the days after the operation, but this should improve day by day.'

After the operation, you can carry on with activities around the house as normal. Avoid eye make-up and try not to get soapy water in your eyes when you wash your hair. If you go out on a windy day, you may feel safer with sunglasses to prevent grit getting in your eye. Your specialist should give you an idea of when you can return to work – this will depend on your recovery.

If you have any concerns, give the eye clinic a call for advice. Brian Little advises, 'Your eyesight will settle down, usually in a few days, although sometimes it can take a week or two. Your vision is often fairly bright and blurred for the first 24 hours, so you should not feel disappointed if your eyesight is not miraculously clear on day one. You will soon find fewer problems with glare and an improvement in your colour vision.'

You will need to have your eyesight tested and may need new glasses. Make an appointment for this a few weeks after the operation – your eye specialist can advise when your eye will have settled. You may need to wait until your spectacles have been updated to start driving again.

New improved lens implants can help you manage without spectacles as ophthalmologist Brian Little explains, 'There are now lens implants available that are "multifocal" and these enable you to see for distance and for reading without the need for glasses. They are not suitable for everybody, but studies have shown that 80-90% of people who have these implants become spectacle independent. Although these lenses are not perfect, they produce a very high level of satisfaction in those who are suited to them. There are also lens implants available that neutralise any naturally occurring astigmatism or irregular curvature of the front of the eye. Unfortunately, none of these are available on the NHS as they are relatively expensive and you are not allowed to make top-up payments.'

In the long term

After some months or years, a minority of people notice that their vision becomes cloudy again in the eye where the cataract has been removed. This is due to clouding of the sac which contains the replacement lens. This cloudiness can be removed with a painless and effective laser treatment in a matter of minutes. Contact your eye specialist if you are concerned that this is happening to you.

If you have had a cataract removed from one eye, it is likely that you will need the same treatment for the other eye at some point in the future.

Case study

'My mother was 84 when she was diagnosed with having cataracts. She was aware of some deterioration in her vision, but we put this down to her age to be honest. She was referred to a consultant at our local hospital. I am my mother's carer, so I accompanied her to the hospital appointment where they put anaesthetic drops into her eyes.

'After this examination, we were given a further appointment to attend day surgery for the removal of the cataract. I took my mother for the procedure and she was able to return home the same day. I did, however, have to care for her for several days; the hospital recommended that she should not be left alone for 24 hours. We were given drops to put into her eye two or three times a day to prevent infection. My mother found it difficult to manage the drops, so once she went back home I arranged for a district nurse to visit her. The nurse was excellent and encouraged my mother to put the drops in herself and managed to get her to independently administer them. Around six weeks later we had a follow-up visit to the hospital where the operation was deemed a success.' Lynn.

Who can help?

Optometrist

An optometrist, also known as an ophthalmic optician, is trained to detect signs of eye disease, as well as measure for and prescribe spectacles. The optometrist can use a light to look for signs of cataracts in your eyes. You can make an appointment with an optometrist at any high street optician.

GP

Your GP is the person who can arrange an appointment at the hospital for you to have your cataract assessed, although many opticians can now refer you directly to hospital.

Ophthalmologist

An ophthalmologist is a doctor who has specialised in eyes. You will be referred to an ophthalmologist for your initial hospital assessment. An ophthalmologist is also the person who will carry out the cataract surgery.

Advice for carers

Cataracts are something that many of us will experience as we get older. If you are caring for someone with a cataract, you can help by:

- Arranging lighting in the home to avoid glare problems (see chapter 8 for more information).
- Accompanying the person to appointments and bringing them home after surgery.

Quick action checklist

- If you suspect that you have a cataract, you should make an appointment for an eye test. It is important to get a professional to check your eye health as blurred vision can have a number of causes.

- If you know that you have a cataract and it is causing problems with your daily life, you should ask your GP for a referral to the hospital eye clinic.

Summing Up

■ A cataract is something most people will experience as they get older and it can be treated.

■ The vast majority of people with a cataract will find that their vision is much improved after surgery. The overall success rate of cataract surgery in the UK is over 95%, and the chances of a serious or sight-threatening complication are less than 1 in 500.

■ After getting your glasses updated, you will be able to carry on with daily life as normal.

Chapter Six

Diabetes and Eye Disease

Diabetes is a common condition where there is too much sugar in the blood. It can be treated, but even with treatment people with diabetes have a higher risk of developing eye problems.

People with diabetes can have eye problems due to leaky or blocked blood vessels in the retina, the layer at the back of the eye. Over time this can cause sight loss. The longer you have diabetes, the more likely you are to develop eye problems. If your diabetes is poorly controlled, this also increases the chance that you will develop diabetic retinopathy (also known as diabetic eye disease). Ophthalmologist Som Prasad adds, 'People with diabetes who control it by managing their diet are also at risk of getting diabetic eye disease and need to get an annual eye check specifically for diabetic retinopathy.'

If you have diabetes you may not notice the signs or symptoms of early diabetic eye problems. You should get your eyes checked regularly to pick up any changes. Som Prasad explains, 'In almost all UK areas, a screening programme will invite you to get an annual eye check using digital photography for diabetic eye disease if you have diabetes. It is extremely important to have this done. Laser treatment of the problem blood vessels can prevent further sight loss for 9 in 10 people, but improvement in sight which has already been lost is only possible for a minority.' Optometrist Nick Rumney suggests, 'If you have not been invited to a screening programme, let your GP know as soon as possible so you can get your eyes checked. You can also make an appointment with an optometrist who can examine your eyes.'

'If you have diabetes, you may not notice the signs or symptoms of early diabetic eye problems. You should get your eyes checked regularly to pick up any changes.'

People with diabetes are twice as likely to develop glaucoma as other adults (see chapter 4 for more information on glaucoma) and also tend to develop cataracts at an earlier age (see chapter 5 for more information on cataracts).

What is diabetes?

When you eat certain foods, your body turns the foods into glucose (sugar). Insulin then helps your body turn the glucose into energy. Diabetes is a condition where there is too much sugar in the blood. This happens because the pancreas doesn't produce enough insulin, or the insulin doesn't have the effect it should.

Food which is converted into glucose includes:

- Carbohydrates, like bread, rice and potatoes.
- Milk and some dairy products.
- Fruit.

Diabetes is relatively common, with between 1.8 and 2.6 million people in the UK being diagnosed with the condition. It is estimated that a further half a million people with the condition have not been diagnosed. Diabetic retinopathy remains the leading cause of glaucoma amongst working-age adults in the UK and most of the developed world.

There are two types of diabetes:

- Type 1 diabetes is when the cells that produce insulin are destroyed by the body, which means you cannot produce any insulin. It usually starts in childhood, and almost always before the age of 40. It is treated by injections of insulin and a healthy diet and lifestyle.
- Type 2 diabetes is when the body doesn't produce enough insulin or the insulin produced is ineffective. It usually starts over the age of 40, but can start from around age 25 in African-Caribbean and South Asian people. It accounts for 17 out of every 20 cases of diabetes. It may be possible to treat with a healthy diet and exercise, but medication and/or insulin may also be needed.

Need2Know

Undetected diabetes causes a number of symptoms. You may:

- Urinate frequently.
- Feel very thirsty.
- Feel very tired.
- Lose weight.
- Have blurred vision.
- Have wounds that heal slowly.
- Have genital itching or thrush.

These problems are caused by high sugar levels. The kidneys try to pass out the extra sugar which can make you urinate more and feel thirsty. You feel tired because your body is not getting the benefit of the food you are eating. The weight loss takes place as the body uses its fat reserves instead. If you have some of these symptoms, you should talk to your GP.

Diabetes and your health

The extra sugar in your system when you have diabetes affects your blood vessels throughout your body. This can cause:

- An increased risk of heart disease, stroke and poor circulation.
- Kidney problems.
- Nerve problems.
- Serious foot problems.
- Impotence.
- Eye problems.

In general, you have a higher risk of problems if your diabetes is poorly controlled. Som Prasad explains, 'The "bad companions" of diabetes, namely high blood pressure, smoking and raised cholesterol, also greatly increase the risk of these types of complications and need to be controlled.'

Why does diabetes cause eye problems?

Raised sugar levels cause changes to blood vessel walls. This is a particular problem in the eye as the blood vessels are small and thin. Diabetic eye disease is the most common complication of diabetes.

Diabetic eye disease develops gradually over time – the longer you have diabetes, the more likely you are to have eye problems. Nearly everyone with Type 1 diabetes will have diabetic eye disease 20 years after their initial diagnosis. Around six people in 10 with Type 2 diabetes show signs of eye disease 20 years after diagnosis.

Who is most at risk?

There are a number of factors that will raise your risk of diabetic eye disease. You have a higher risk of diabetic eye disease if you are diabetic and:

- You have had diabetes for a long time. It is uncommon in people who have had diabetes for less than five years, but almost everyone who has had diabetes for over 30 years has signs of eye disease.

- Your diabetes is not well controlled. However, some people with well-controlled diabetes will still develop diabetic eye disease.

- You have high blood pressure that is not well controlled.

- You have diabetic kidney disease (known as nephropathy).

- You are pregnant, particularly if your diabetes is poorly controlled.

- You smoke.

- You are obese.

- You have high cholesterol.

What happens inside the eyes?

Diabetic eye disease starts with small changes to the blood vessels at the back of the eye. You can't see these changes yourself but an eye specialist can detect them when using a bright light to look inside your eye. There is a national screening programme where digital photos of the back of your eye are taken regularly so specialists can detect any early changes.

Initially, tiny swellings appear in the walls of the blood vessels that carry nutrients to the retina. These swellings are known as 'microaneurysms'. Fluid can leak through the weak blood vessels, which can be a clear fluid leak or a leak of blood. At this early stage, known as 'background diabetic retinopathy', there is no threat to your sight, but it is still important to attend your appointments, as advised by your specialist, to monitor the condition.

After these initial swellings, some of the retinal blood vessels can become blocked, leading to parts of the retina becoming deprived of blood. The retina then sends out signals to the body to grow new blood vessels, but these new vessels are fragile. They grow and attach themselves to the surface of the gel inside the eye but leak easily, causing scar tissue to form which is what leads to severe vision loss. This is known as 'proliferative diabetic retinopathy'.

Macular problems

People with diabetes can have problems with the macula, the central part of the retina that allows you to see small details.

Diabetic retinopathy that involves the macula can cause problems with your central vision.

The leaky blood vessels in the retina can also cause extra fluid to leak into the macula which makes it swell – this makes vision blurred. It can happen at any time but is more likely to happen if you have had diabetes for a long time. If you have diabetes and your vision becomes blurred, you should contact your diabetic specialist immediately.

'Diabetic eye disease starts with small changes to the blood vessels at the back of the eye. You can't see these changes yourself but an eye specialist can detect them when using a bright light to look inside your eye.'

Detecting diabetic eye problems

If you know you have diabetes, you should be invited to a special eye test at least every year. How often you are offered an appointment will depend on your own particular circumstances. Some people attend a diabetic eye check at normal high street opticians, while others may be seen in a hospital clinic or community screening centre. When you go for a screening appointment, your eye specialist will:

- Check your level of vision.

- Check the pressure inside the eye. This will be done either using a small probe that rests on the eye or a machine that sends out a puff of air. Checking the pressure helps the practitioner look for developing glaucoma.

- Give you some eye drops which will dilate your pupil, allowing the eye specialist to get a really good view of the back of the eye. Your eye care professional will then shine a bright light into the eye to check the tiny blood vessels on the retina. This may be dazzling but isn't painful.

- Take a photograph of the back of the eye. This gives your specialist the ability to more easily compare changes at the back of the eye, year on year.

After the tests your eyesight will be blurred until the drops wear off. You will have to arrange an alternative way home as you won't be able to drive.

Read more about the national programme for diabetic eye checks at www. retinalscreening.nhs.uk.

Further tests

If the eye specialist suspects certain problems, they may refer you for further tests. A test called a 'fluorescein angiogram' uses dye to show up leaky blood vessels at the back of the eye. In this procedure, eye drops are used to get a clear view of the back of your eyes, while a special dye is injected into your arm and photos are taken as the dye passes through the blood vessels at the back of the eye. The eye specialist will be able to see where fluid or blood is leaking at the back of the eye.

Treatment for diabetic eye problems

If mild or early diabetic eye disease is detected, you are unlikely to be offered treatment. Instead, your eyes will be monitored every few months.

Laser treatment

If you have new blood vessels growing at the back of the eye, laser treatment is used to treat them. Laser treatment can usually prevent diabetic eye disease from getting worse or at least slow down the rate of further visual loss. However, it can only occasionally restore lost sight. If you are offered laser treatment, bear in mind you may need more than one treatment session.

- You will attend your appointment for laser treatment at an outpatients clinic and you won't need to stay overnight in hospital.

- The specialist will give you some eye drops to widen your pupil so they can see the back of the eye in detail. More drops will numb the surface of the eye and a contact lens will be put onto the eye's surface.

- The specialist administering the laser treatment will focus the laser on problem areas at the back of the eye and make tiny burns. This is done to seal leaks and prevent new blood vessel growth.

- The treatment may be uncomfortable, but only some types of treatment cause pain. The specialist will tell you if you are likely to need pain relief.

After laser treatment

Because the laser is very bright, your vision will be blurred immediately after the operation and you may also have a headache. Some people also notice that they have some black spots on their vision after treatment.

If you have laser treatment, your peripheral vision can be affected, so you must let the Driver and Vehicle Licensing Agency (DVLA) know when you have had the treatment.

'Laser treatment can usually prevent diabetic eye disease from getting worse or at least slow down the rate of further visual loss. However, it can only occasionally restore lost sight.'

New treatments

Newer treatments, including injection of steroid preparation or anti-VEGF (vascular endothelial growth factor) into the gel in the back of the eye, are being explored and may be offered to you if appropriate.

Other treatments

- If your specialist has spotted changes to the macula, you will be offered laser treatment.
- If you have a bleed into the gel in the eye, you may need surgery. The bleed can cause scar tissue and sight loss, so it can be necessary to remove the gel.
- For a small number of people, the growth of new fragile blood vessels can cause the retina to become detached. You would then need surgery to reattach the retina.

'You should discuss any treatment with your eye specialist. Don't be afraid to ask for clarification if there's anything you don't understand.'

You should discuss any treatment with your eye specialist. Don't be afraid to ask for clarification if there's anything you don't understand. There is a leaflet about treatment available to download from www.retinalscreening.nhs.uk.

Diabetic eye disease and sight loss

If, despite treatment, you experience sight loss due to diabetic eye disease, your eye specialist will be able to advise you on making the most of your sight. Read chapters 7 and 8 for more information on magnifiers, better lighting and help at home and outdoors.

What can I do to look after my eyes?

If you have diabetes, there are a number of things you can do to minimise sight problems:

- Attend a regular eye check every year, or more often if advised by your specialist.

- Take care to control your blood sugar as well as possible. This can delay the start of eye problems, slow their progression and reduce the need for laser surgery. Talk to your GP about controlling your diabetes.

- For adults, looking after your blood pressure and cholesterol can also reduce the risk of sight loss. Again, get medical advice to help with this.

- Do not smoke as this can add to problems. If you smoke, speak to your GP or pharmacist about getting help to stop.

- Exercise regularly and aim to lose any extra weight. If you have problems losing weight, ask your GP for a referral to a dietitian. If you need help getting fit, ask about exercise programmes in your local health centre.

- If you notice an increase in spots floating in your vision or your vision becomes blurred, contact your specialist as soon as possible.

Advice for carers

If you live with or care for someone with diabetes, there are a number of things you can do to help. On a day-to-day basis:

- Encourage them to eat a healthy diet, plenty of fruit, veg and wholegrains. For more information, see *Food for Health – The Essential Guide* (Need2Know).

- Encourage them take part in exercise. Perhaps do something together or have a look in your local area for classes or clubs.

- Ensure they attend their regular eye checks.

- Encourage them to manage their diabetes to stay in good general health.

Quick action checklist

- If you have diabetes, the most important thing is to attend regular eye checks – annually or more often if advised.

- Aim for the best blood sugar control that you can. Speak to your GP or diabetes specialist nurse if you need help with this.

- Look after your blood pressure and cholesterol level. Your GP will be able to give you advice on this.

- Think about improving your lifestyle. Aim to increase your regular exercise, lose excess weight and/or stop smoking.

Summing Up

■ Diabetes is a common condition which can cause problems inside the eye. These changes, known as diabetic retinopathy or diabetic eye disease, can lead to sight loss.

■ Good control of diabetes can slow the development of diabetic eye problems. Regular eye checks can pick up problems before you develop serious sight loss. If there are signs of diabetic eye disease which need treating, laser treatment can prevent further sight loss.

■ Anyone with diabetes can look after their eyes and cut the risk of eye problems by eating healthily, exercising and managing their diabetes.

Chapter Seven

Mobility When Out and About

If your sight is getting worse, the outside world can seem like a frightening place full of obstacles to negotiate. You may no longer be able to drive and lack confidence in negotiating public transport. While you may not be able to do everything you once could, there is support available to help you keep your independence and social life.

- Mobility training can help you learn new ways to feel confident out and about.

- Support groups and voluntary organisations can offer help and interesting activities and holidays.

Mobility training

If you are struggling to cope with getting out and about, mobility training can help. Ask your hospital eye department if they can put you in touch with your local rehabilitation team, or find them through your local authority's social care department. Your local social care department has a duty to assess your need, but they may not offer training. However, they should be able to refer you to a local provider for training. The charity Guide Dogs (also known as The Guide Dogs for the Blind Association) also has rehabilitation officers who can come to your home.

'Mobility training can help you learn new ways to feel confident out and about.'

Who can help?

If you are experiencing sight loss, a rehabilitation officer can help you get to grips with everyday activities again. A rehabilitation officer is often based in the community and they will assess what your needs are and either offer you appropriate assistance and training or refer you to an organisation that provides what you need.

Virtually every council will have access to a sensory rehabilitation team. However, staffing levels vary in different areas and there are shortages of trained rehabilitation officers. The work is often contracted out to local voluntary associations for blind people.

When assessing you and your needs, a rehabilitation officer will look at:

- Your daily routine.

- How you are managing when out and about.

- How you use the sight that you have.

- Methods of communication including reading, using computers or learning Braille or Moon.

- The lighting in your home.

- Aids and equipment which may help you.

- How you manage everyday tasks in the home.

A rehabilitation officer will come to you at home and listen to you explaining your mobility needs. They can offer:

- Advice on equipment to help with mobility, such as canes.

- Mobility training to help you learn to use a cane effectively.

- Help and training for people who guide you.

Optometrist Nick Rumney says, 'In my opinion, sighted guide training is almost the most important and most overlooked rehabilitation help available.'

The rehabilitation officer will want to find out about:

- Any difficulties you are having.

- How often you go out independently.

- Which routes you can manage independently.

- Where you would like to go independently.

- How you usually travel – by foot, bus, train, tram or car.

They will also ask about your use of different clues to help you get out and about. These include:

- Sound clues, e.g. traffic noise, end of building lines and sound shadows.

- Visual clues, e.g. contrast, shapes and colours.

- Tactile clues, e.g. a change of surface or tactile paving.

Don't worry if you don't think you use these clues, you may actually be doing it without being aware of it. The rehabilitation officer can assess you if you go out together.

The rehabilitation officer will also ask questions about how much you can see. Tell them about the sight you have in each eye, and whether you have problems with glare, difficulties seeing in dim light or problems moving from dark to light areas.

Before your assessment, have a think about whether you can see the following and at what distance:

- Street signs.

- Bus numbers.

- Kerbs.

- Traffic lights.

- Moving traffic.

- Controlled crossings.

- Side roads.

- Main roads.

Your training

If you are invited to a mobility training course, you will be shown simple techniques to make it easier to do day-to-day things like:

- Navigate stairs.
- Find your way outdoors.
- Cross the road safely.
- Get on and off buses and trains.

The rehabilitation officer will work with you in and around your own home; following routes that you take regularly and helping you gain confidence on new routes that you need to know.

A course may take place over a set number of weeks, or you may work with a rehabilitation officer over a period of anything from a month up to a year to develop your skills.

Using a cane

There are many different sorts of cane. Some simply show that you have sight loss and act as a sign to other people. Other canes can help you navigate obstacles, and you will need training to use this sort of cane. If you need a walking stick already, you can opt for a white stick to show people you have sight problems.

Symbol canes

A symbol cane is a lightweight folding or telescopic white cane that simply shows others that you have some sight loss. It isn't strong enough to support you. If you have some useful vision, a symbol cane may enable you to go out independently, and it can also be carried if you are being guided. The symbol cane can be folded up and put in your bag when you have reached your destination.

Guide canes

This sort of cane is carried diagonally across your body, pointing at the floor. It can be used to scan for hazards like steps and kerbs. White in colour, this type of cane is lightweight to make it easier to carry, but it won't support your weight. Canes vary in length, and a rehabilitation officer may be able to help you choose the right one for you. If choosing for yourself, pick a cane that reaches from just above your waist to the floor.

Long canes

You can learn to use a long cane on a mobility training course. This can allow you to travel independently, even if you have no useful vision.

A long cane's length will depend on your height and length of stride. You can learn to tap from side to side, to 'sweep' an area clear of obstacles before you take your next step. You are taught to tap across the width of your body so you step into the place where you just tapped. Alternatively, the long cane can be fitted with a different type of tip and you can learn a 'rolling' technique to check for obstacles.

Long cane techniques will help you detect obstacles and kerbs, but they will only pick up those below waist height. Learning this sort of technique will take time – some people pick it up in a couple of weeks, while others need up to 10 training sessions.

You will benefit from expert support to master using a long cane. Ask your rehabilitation officer if a long cane would help with your mobility. Your rehabilitation worker can help you learn a specific route with a long cane.

'Long cane techniques will help you detect obstacles and kerbs, but they will only pick up those below waist height.'

Walking sticks

If you need to use a stick to help you walk, a white painted walking stick in aluminium or wood can also make people aware that you have sight loss. If you choose to use a walking stick to support your mobility, you should ensure that an occupational therapist or physiotherapist assesses you to make sure that the stick is the correct height.

If you are using a cane to help with mobility, it is useful to know that there are different sorts of cane tip available too. RNIB has a leaflet with specific advice on different tip types for different techniques and canes; see *Choosing Cane Tips*.

Guide dogs

A guide dog can help you with your mobility and confidence when out and about. Guide dogs are available for people of any age and with varying amounts of sight loss. Nick Rumney adds, 'Only about 3% of blind people have the sort of vision/lifestyle to warrant a guide dog.'

Guide Dogs (see help list) can supply dogs, training and ongoing help with the cost of food and vets bills if needed. If you are interested, you can call and arrange for someone to come and talk to you about getting a guide dog. They will help you explore whether a dog is your best option and offer advice on other ways to improve your mobility. The member of staff from your Guide Dogs district team will assess your lifestyle to see whether you need an active dog that enjoys being out and about or one that is happy with a more sedentary lifestyle. Remember that dogs do need regular exercise.

If you decide to apply for a dog and you are assessed as being suitable, there may be a wait until the right dog for you is found. Different dogs suit different people and it is important to get one that is right for your level of activity and lifestyle. You will then be invited to meet the dog and their instructor. You and your new dog will spend four weeks attending a training school each day, where you can learn to work as a partnership. Once you have qualified, you can get continuing support from your district team at Guide Dogs.

More about getting out and about

Some areas offer reduced fares for public transport and you may be able to access the Blue Badge Scheme as described in chapter 9.

Wearing protective eyewear can really help with the glare from UV rays and also help to increase your mobility. RNIB have a selection of eye shields to choose from and can offer advice on selecting the right pair for your needs.

Shopping

It can seem daunting if you have sight problems and want to go shopping. There are a number of ways to get help:

- Big stores often have someone who can help you – call in advance to find out if your local supermarket offers this service. Some stores offer telephone ordering and delivery services too.

- Look into local voluntary organisations. They may offer volunteers who can assist you with your shopping.

- If you are shopping with someone, you'll need to explain exactly what you need. Maybe you can make a shopping list with the person who you are going out with. Use a bold black marker if this allows you to see the list too.

- Tell the person helping you with your shopping about the brands you like, and ask them to point out special offers if they might interest you.

Leisure, sports and staying active

If your sight is deteriorating, you'll need to take action to ensure that you stay fit and still get to take part in enjoyable and social leisure activities. You might enjoy taking up bowling or joining a local walking group. Look for groups that arrange tours round towns or gentle rambles through the countryside. Walking for Health can help you find walking groups near you (see help list).

Getting out and active can help you feel better physically but also has emotional benefits. Exercise creates feel-good hormones and can help you feel more positive, plus you will meet new people and get to know them during your shared activity.

Holidays

If your sight is worsening, you may be able to cope at home but find the thought of getting away for a break quite daunting. There are a number of organisations that can help.

'Look into local voluntary organisations. They may offer volunteers who can assist you with your shopping.'

- Action for Blind People has a number of hotels (see Vision Hotels in the help list) across the UK, by the sea and in the countryside.

- Vitalise Holidays offers group holidays in the UK and worldwide for visually impaired adults. You will be supported throughout your holiday by Vitalise sighted guides, and can choose from activity-based holidays, trips to London shows, or simply a break in the sun. All holidays are graded so you can choose an easy holiday or an energetic break.

- Access at Last offers information on accessible accommodation worldwide.

- Torch Holiday and Retreat Centre offers holidays at Hurstpierpoint in Sussex. The centre uses attractive high contrast colour schemes to help you get around independently.

- Traveleyes was founded by Amar Latif after he experienced the limitations of travelling as a person with a visual impairment. The company offers trips through Europe, Africa and the Americas.

- Vision Outdoor is a German company offering tours in Europe and beyond. You can opt to book assistance as part of the holiday. Themed breaks on offer include wine tasting, canoeing and hiking.

Advice for carers

For anyone losing their sight, going out of the house can become challenging. You can help them by:

- Being aware that every person with sight loss is an individual. Think about how the help that you give will enable them to move towards greater independence.

- Offering help, but don't take responsibility.

- Encouraging a dialogue and work in partnership. If you are guiding someone, it may be easier for them to hold a door open if it is on their side, for example.

- Contacting Guide Dogs for their DVD on being a sighted guide for lots more tips.

Quick action checklist

If you want to get out and about more, here are some good starting points:

- Find out who offers rehabilitation services in your area. Ask your hospital eye clinic, social worker, GP, or contact your local association for blind people.

- Call Guide Dogs. Their rehabilitation officers can offer advice and help with mobility, whether or not you are suitable for a guide dog.

- Think about how much exercise you do. Start looking around for a group to join so you can stay fit and active.

- Ask local voluntary organisations or contact your local big stores to find out if there is any help you can access for shopping.

- If you want to be a bit more adventurous, look into options for holidays.

Summing Up

- It can seem like your world is closing in when your sight is getting worse and you can no longer be as independent as you used to be. A rehabilitation officer can help you regain your confidence and independence to get out and about again.

- Speak to your rehabilitation officer about whether a cane or guide dog might be the right mobility aid for you – different aids suit different people. Whatever you opt for, remember that training will use the aid effectively and help you stay safe.

- Think about what else you would like to do. If you want to get out to the shops, start researching who might be able to help you. If are feeling down or putting on weight, make finding a friendly group to exercise with a priority.

- Then, if you want to expand your horizons as you get more confident, look into booking a holiday. With specialist tour providers and holiday companies, your sight loss is no barrier to exploring the world.

Chapter Eight

Help Around the Home

If your sight is getting worse you may be worried about how you'll cope at home. This chapter is packed with practical tips on how to adjust your home and routine and how to get hold of aids to make life easier.

RNIB is the first point of call for all sorts of practical aids and advice. It has 13 resource centres across England, Scotland, Northern Ireland and the Isle of Man where you can view and buy products to help you.

In this chapter we also look at how good lighting and contrast can make it easier for you to see things using the vision that you have. Remember, 'bigger, bolder, brighter' are all ways to make it easier for you at home.

Staying in your home

If you are finding it hard to navigate your home, there are some simple yet practical things that can help.

Using contrast

Increasing contrast can make things much easier to see. Compare searching for something black on a white background with looking for a grey object on a grey surface. This idea can make your home much easier and safer to live in. Use a contrasting colour for:

- Door handles – paint them, use tape or change for a different colour door handle.

- Doors – paint the door in contrast to the frame and walls.

'Local voluntary societies for people with sight loss also have resource centres. See if you can find one in your area.'

Stephen Kill, rehabilitation officer and eye 2 eye manager for SeeAbility.

- Edges of steps – mark with white paint or use white plastic or metal strips known as 'nosings'.

- The banister on your stairs – paint this a colour that stands out from the surrounding colours.

- Cupboard door edges – this could save you from a bump if the door is open.

- Glass doors – stick some bright transfers or stickers to any glass doors around your home.

'If you find it difficult to move from bright areas to darker ones or vice versa, try to adjust the light levels in your home so that it is evenly bright, or at least so there are no very dark or dim areas.'

Lighting

Good lighting makes an enormous difference to how well you can see things at home. During the day make the most of daylight. For most people, good daylight is easier to see in than any sort of artificial light.

- Pull the curtains right back to make the most of daylight.

- Clean your windows regularly and opt for light coloured walls and woodwork.

- Check the power of your light bulbs and consider if you can safely increase the wattage of light bulb.

- Add more lights – use an angle poise light shining from over your left shoulder onto your task, or position the light between you and the task for maximum benefit. Place it so it is as close to the task as practical, but make sure it isn't placed so it could burn you.

Other lighting ideas

RNIB advises, 'Before using higher wattage bulbs, you should check that the type of bulb is safe for the fittings and shades that you currently have. If in doubt, you should ask an electrician to check for you.'

- If you find it difficult to move from bright areas to darker ones or vice versa, try to adjust the light levels in your home so that it is evenly bright, or at least so there are no very dark or dim areas. You may need to increase the number of lights in some areas or increase the wattage of the bulbs you use in others.

80

- If bright lights make it harder for you to see, you may want to switch off overhead lighting and just use 'task lighting' to focus on things you need to see. Dimmer switches can allow you to adjust light to the right level for you.

- Problems with glare can also make it harder than necessary for you to see. Start with large sunglasses: some styles have a plastic ridge that stops light coming in through the top and shields that prevent light entering through the sides. Over glasses or 'over shields' fit over your spectacles and are available from the RNIB shop. Add in a hat or visor for additional protection.

- If your home has stairs, it is important to keep them well lit. Make sure that you can switch lights off and on at both the top and the bottom of the stairs. Watch out for energy saving light bulbs as these can take time to reach their full brightness and may not be suitable for stairs and hallways. See the RNIB leaflet *See for Yourself* for more advice on different types of lighting and light bulbs.

- Put tape round light switches and sockets if they are a similar colour to the wall. Or, you may want to contact an electrician about fitting switches and sockets in a contrasting colour. While doing this, think about whether you might find it easier if sockets are raised rather than at floor level.

If you're redecorating

Think about your walls and floors when you next come to redecorate, as this can make it easier for you.

- Use light colours to reflect light and make rooms brighter. Watch out for white though, as this can cause glare. Choose matt paint instead of gloss to cut down glare.

- Avoid hectic patterns as it can be hard to see things against them. Introduce pattern and personality with your cushions and curtains rather than with the wallpaper.

- If you need to navigate down a corridor or hall, use a border or even a rail at hand height which you can follow.

- Choose carpet or tiles in a contrasting colour to the walls. Then opt for skirting in a contrasting colour too.

Your kitchen

Cooking for yourself can seem important in so many ways. You might want to be able to make a hot drink for yourself at a time that suits you, or be able to go to the fridge and find what you need for your favourite meal. Fortunately, there are lots of ways to make using the kitchen easier.

Use colour contrast to help you cook food safely. Put tape along the edge of shelves and work surfaces in a contrasting colour. Use mats or chopping boards in contrasting colours to make kitchen equipment stand out. It is easier to cut up light coloured food on a dark board and vice versa. RNIB and local voluntary association resource centres sell a range of easy-to-see kitchen products such as:

- Talking kitchen scales.
- Talking measuring jugs.
- Big, bold timers.
- Non-slip mats.
- Contrasting chopping boards.
- Liquid level indicators which tell you when a cup or jug is nearly full.
- Talking microwaves and scales.

Visit the cooking section in the RNIB online shop or go to one of their resource centres where you can see and try a range of products.

Labelling

There are good ways to help you know what food you have in your fridge and store cupboards. RNIB advises, 'There are many different ways of labelling items. You can put a rubber band around your toothbrush to distinguish it from someone else's, place magnetic letters onto tin lids or make clear print labels using thick, dark felt tip pens. Braille labels can easily be made and you can create personalised audible labels.'

Here are some more ideas for labelling available from RNIB:

- Bumpons are sheets of self-adhesive bumps. You can choose different sizes and colours and use them to create a code to label food as well as to indicate the 'on' and 'off' positions on the washing machine dial or microwave.

- Talking tins can record an audio description and attach to the relevant tin so you can play it back when you're looking for something in the cupboard.

- Tactimark is a liquid plastic that you can use to write on storage tins. It dries leaving a raised line, and is available in black, white and orange.

Whatever labelling system you choose, ask someone to go through your food with you when you get back from the shop and put on the labels that work for you.

Ask in the local library for large print cookbooks, and contact your rehabilitation officer to find out if they can offer help so you can develop your kitchen skills to cook safely.

Kitchen lighting

Often when you are cooking at a kitchen work surface, your body can be between the ceiling light and the surface – meaning that you don't get the benefit from the light. Add a light under a cupboard or on a shelf that shines onto where you work to make it a bit easier to do kitchen activities. Try a clip-on spotlight to see where you get the best effect.

Your bathroom

If you are concerned about safety in the bathroom, there are some simple things to do to make it safer and easier to use.

- Think about grab rails – these work well to help you get in and out of the bath and shower. Look for ones which contrast with the wall, or mark the rails with waterproof tape.

- As in the kitchen, bright and contrasting accessories can be easier to find and use – this applies to toilet roll holders and soap dishes, as well as the toilet roll and soap itself.

- A toilet seat in a contrasting colour can make a big difference too – if you have a white toilet, choose a dark seat.

- If you are refitting the bathroom, choose non-slip flooring. Matt wall tiles are less slippery too. You can use contrasting colours to make it easier to see where you are in the room.

Telephones

Large button and large print telephones can make it easier for you to use the telephone. There are also large button mobile phones with bigger displays and one model of talking mobile phone. Plus, some phones are compatible with software to make it easier to use. RNIB offers a factsheet which covers current models, functions and costs. Rehabilitation officer Stephen Kill advises, 'Memory buttons are also useful to help you dial numbers you use regularly.'

Magnifiers for practical tasks

A magnifier can make it easier to see dials and switches, check labels and read letters and bills. You will benefit from getting advice and trying a range of magnifiers. Contact your local low vision service or rehabilitation officer as a starting point if you want to try out magnifiers. Proper help and training can make it much easier for you to use a magnifier.

Magnifiers for close up

Magnifiers come in different strengths. Unfortunately, the magnification amount is not properly standardised so although ×4 means that it magnifies things by a factor of 4, this is only true if it is held in a particular way. Ask your optometrist or low vision aid supplier to help you work out which is the correct one for the task in hand. There are slightly different ways of calculating magnifier strength, so you will benefit from being shown which power is best for what sort of tasks and how to use it.

Different magnifiers suit different tasks. With stronger magnifiers, you may only see part of a word at a time. It is important to work out the distance from your eyes to the magnifier and the distance from the magnifier to the task where you get most benefit. This is why it is best the magnifier is prescribed by a professional who can advise you. The stronger the magnifier, the closer you may have to work – which can be tiring to your posture.

'You do not need to buy a magnifier because they are available free of charge through low vision clinics. Ask your optometrist, optician, ophthalmologist or GP to refer you.'

Nick Rumney, optometrist.

Get the right lighting to help you when using a magnifier. Use a light that you can shine onto the print you want to read, ideally one with adjustable position for maximum benefit.

Different types of magnifier include:

- Hand held – available in ×1.5 to ×11 (+3DS to +40DS). Can include a battery powered light, but may be difficult to use if you have weak hands.

- Stand magnifiers – these are good if you need your hands free, to write or sew for instance. Available from ×2 to ×20 (+4DS to +80DS) and can also come with an integral light.

- Pocket magnifiers – these are small, sometimes folding, and mainly useful for out and about. Available from ×2 to ×15 (+4DS to +60DS).

- Spectacle magnifiers – these attach to your spectacles and can be very powerful. They also offer the widest possible field of view, but you will need special instructions to use them because of the close distances needed.

All these sorts of magnifiers should be available to try on loan from your local low vision service – contact your hospital eye department for details. Rehabilitation officer, Stephen Kill stresses, 'Assessment for these aids is essential to ensure that you get the right aid for the right activity.'

Electronic low vision devices

You can also get benefits from a number of electronic magnifying devices.

- CCTVs (closed-circuit TVs) use a special camera to make the print you want to read appear on a TV screen or a monitor. You can adjust the magnification and contrast, magnifying it by as much as ×70.

- CCTV readers are hand-held camera devices that you move across the page. Some can plug into your TV.

You are unlikely to be able to get these on loan, but the RNIB can help you find schemes and grants to obtain one, plus it offers a factsheet on CCTVs. The Macular Disease Society also has a list of second-hand CCTVs for sale (see help list).

'Assessment for these aids is essential to ensure that you get the right aid for the right activity.'

Stephen Kill, rehabilitation officer and eye 2 eye manager for SeeAbility.

For distance viewing

You may find a monocular or binocular useful for watching TV. A monocular can magnify things by ×2.5 to ×14. You need to get advice from your low vision service on whether a monocular will suit you and how to use it to best effect. It can take practise to get it right.

RNIB's hints and tips for using magnifiers

- Hand magnifiers usually work best with distance spectacles, stand magnifiers usually work best with reading glasses. Use the pair of spectacles that the low vision service recommends. If in doubt as to which pair to use, contact your low vision service or optician.

- If you use a magnifier to make print bigger, you can often only see one or two words or letters at a time. You can reduce this effect by having the magnifier as close to your eye as possible and arranging the text to be at the correct focused distance. Do not hold a magnifier at arm's length! This can make it hard to keep your place. Try using your finger to mark each line. When reaching the end of a line, return to the beginning of the line with your finger before dropping down onto the next one.

- Holding a magnifier close to your eye and bringing what you want to see up to it will often help you see more letters and words at a time.

- Some people find moving the book or page from side to side easier than moving the magnifier or their eyes.

- If you are using your magnifier to read when sitting in a chair, put the book or newspaper you are reading on a clipboard to help keep the page flat and still. A cushion or a tray may be useful to provide support.

- Keep your magnifier clean by using a lens cleaner (available from most opticians), or use warm, soapy water and dry with a soft cloth.

- Use different magnifiers for different tasks.

- If you find your eyes are getting tired, take a break and start again when you feel better.

'If you find your eyes are getting tired, take a break and start again when you feel better.'

- If you are having problems using your magnifier, get in touch with your local low vision service. They may be able to give you more training or swap it for another one.

Reproduced with permission of Royal National Institute of Blind People (RNIB). Extract from *See for Yourself*, © RNIB 2010. Visit www.rnib.org.uk/livingwithsightloss for more information.

Reading

Reading is something that you do every day, from checking a label on a tin to sitting down with a good book. There are ways to make this easier, working with the level of sight that you have. For example, if there is something in particular that you need to read – be it instructions or a knitting pattern – you could enlarge it using a photocopier. For other ways to enjoy reading:

- Get advice about good magnifiers from your eye specialist so you can continue to read regular books.

- Find out about large print and talking books, your local library may have some.

- RNIB's book site catalogue contains over 20,000 audio and Braille books, Braille music manuscripts and accessible maps. You can register on http://booksite.rnib.org.uk to buy books or subscribe annually to listen to any of the 12,000 Daisy audio book titles via your computer.

'Find out about large print and talking books, your local library may have some.'

Writing

If you need to write anything down, be it a note for the milkman or a shopping list, there are a few things you can do to make it easier:

- Set yourself up at a desk with a black marker pen and a large piece of paper – this makes it easier for you to read back what you have written.

- Use an adjustable lamp to shine light directly onto your paper.

- If you have problems writing along a straight line, use a writing frame. This could simply be a slot cut into a piece of card: rest the card on your paper and write within the slot.

- Try to find some thick lined paper if possible.

Using a computer

Think about the location of your computer carefully so you don't get glare from nearby windows. It usually works best if you avoid facing a window or sitting in front of a window. Instead, try setting up the screen side-on to any windows.

There are lots of accessibility features included on modern computers. Ask someone to look at the settings for you to see if there are any options that would make it easier for you to use the computer.

- You may find it easier to work with light text on a dark background or dark text on a light background.
- Changing the background from white to yellow can cut glare.
- Adjust the viewing size on your computer as this can make everything larger.
- Use large, clear fonts to create documents.
- Find out about software that will read text back to you and speech packages which will read a document out to you.
- There are keyboard covers available with large print letters or you could use stickers to customise your keyboard.

'Audio description services have a narrator providing extra commentary about the background scenery, expressions and movement, to make sure that you miss as little as possible.'

Watching TV

There are ways to ensure that you can still enjoy TV, whatever your level of sight. Starting simply, try moving your chair a bit closer to the TV and make sure that the lighting doesn't cause glare by positioning your TV away from the window.

Audio description services have a narrator providing extra commentary about the background scenery, expressions and movement, to make sure that you miss as little as possible. You can find audio description services on TV and DVDs as well as in cinemas, theatres and other venues.

RNIB runs Insight Radio, providing a dedicated service tailored to listeners with sight loss. Programmes are broadcast on Sky channel 0188, freesat channel 777 and via http://insightradio.co.uk.

Advice for carers

Sight loss can be frustrating, but with the right help people can continue to enjoy hobbies and look after themselves at home.

■ You could contact RNIB or your local voluntary association for blind people to find out if there is a resource centre close by. Resource centres are a great place to try out products and get advice on what products could help and how much they cost.

■ Good lighting is really important to help people make the most of their sight. Go around the house with the person you support and talk about where they might benefit from better light. You may need to alter the light bulbs, buy an additional clip on or angle poise light or get advice from an electrician.

Quick action checklist

Look at your home and work through the following to see how things could be better for you:

■ Do you need to update your decor to make things easier to see? Remember: plain, light walls, with contrast colours for switches, doors and even a guide rail can all help make day-to-day life easier.

■ Lighting makes a big difference to your home. Take each of the rooms in your house in turn and, one at a time, think about how the lighting could be better.

■ Cooking for yourself can help you to be independent. Think about what you'd like to be able to do and contact your rehabilitation officer to see if they can help. You can find a rehabilitation officer through your local social care department or your local voluntary association for blind people.

■ Different magnifiers suit different people and situations. You may benefit from having more than one sort. Get expert advice from an optometrist or rehabilitation officer.

Summing Up

- One of the key frustrations of sight loss can be losing the ability to do things at home. Whether you want to cook for yourself, keep up a hobby or just enjoy TV again there are lots of resources to help.

- Remember that if you make things bigger, bolder and brighter, they can be easier to see.

- Colour contrast can help as well. You may simply want to buy different coloured soap or toilet paper to see more easily in the bathroom, or get some coloured mats and plates to increase colour contrast in the kitchen and dining rooms.

- A rehabilitation officer can help you relearn skills. You can still enjoy your pastimes and hobbies. Speak to your rehabilitation officer about what you like to do and they can advise you on the best magnifiers, aids and lighting for the job.

- You may also want to call on the skills of a local decorator or electrician if you want to make adaptations to your home.

Chapter Nine

Financial Help

Living with sight loss can cause extra expense – for example, trips to the hospital or specially adapted aids that you may have to buy. However, many people with sight loss are not accessing the financial support that they are entitled to. There are a number of grants and other financial help available to help to relieve some of the strain. This chapter will:

- Help you identify what benefits can be claimed when you have sight loss and also what grants are on offer.

- Offer straightforward advice about how to manage your money and avoid or cope with debt.

- Explore your rights at work, offer advice on how to find work and how the Disability Discrimination Act can support you in your workplace.

Benefits

There are a number of different benefits that you may be entitled to claim depending on your age and circumstances. It's important that you keep up to date with what benefits are on offer to make sure that you are always claiming what you are entitled to. RNIB has a helpline that you can call in order to check that you are receiving all of the correct benefits (see help list). Directgov (see help list) has a 'benefits advisor' section where you can answer a series of questions anonymously in order to find out which benefits you may be able to claim.

There is no specific benefit for people who have sight loss, as mentioned in chapter 1, although people registered as blind or partially sighted can get discounts through the Disabled Person's Railcard, access to the Blue Badge Scheme and discounted TV licence fees. Anyone registered blind also gets a tax allowance worth £1,890 (at the time of going to press) whatever their age or income. You can also get free NHS sight tests – even if you have sight problems, your eyes still need a regular check-up and you may continue to benefit from an up-to-date spectacle prescription.

Attendance Allowance

Attendance Allowance is for people aged 65 or over who need help with their personal care. It is not means tested so any income or savings that you have will not be taken into account. RNIB has compiled an Attendance Allowance support pack to help with filling in the forms – you can contact the helpline to get a copy.

Carer's Allowance

In order for your carer to claim Carer's Allowance, you must be claiming the Attendance Allowance payments or the middle or high rate of the Disability Living Allowance.

Plus, in order to qualify as a carer, your carer must perform caring duties for at least 35 hours each week. They should be over 16 years old and must not be attending a course for over 21 hours each week. There are also criteria regarding how much the carer can earn and still be eligible for Carer's Allowance. For the most up-to-date information and to download an application form, visit www.direct.gov.uk.

Disability Living Allowance

Disability Living Allowance (DLA) is for people who need help with their care and/or mobility. In order to qualify for this benefit, you must be under 65 when you make your claim. It is made up of two components, care and mobility, and you can make a claim under both components if appropriate. The care component has three different weekly rates depending on whether low, medium or high levels of care are needed and the mobility component has either a low or high weekly component.

In order to claim DLA, you will need to telephone the Benefit Enquiry Line for a claim pack (they are available in large print but you will need to request this format). You can also ask for help with completing the pack: the telephone number for help can be found at the end of this book. Action for Blind People has a helpful factsheet to assist you in including all the right information for your claim which can be downloaded from their website (see help list).

Housing Benefit and Council Tax Benefit

These two benefits can help to pay all or part of your rent or council tax. Both benefits are means tested and are awarded by your local authority – they will be able to provide you with an application form. Your sight difficulties may mean that you are eligible for the Council Tax Benefits Disability Reduction Scheme. In order to qualify, there are certain conditions, for example, the person with sight problems must have a permanent disability and it must be of a substantial nature. They should also require extra space or adaptations within the home in order to accommodate their needs.

Pension Credit

If you are over 60 and have a low income, you may qualify for this benefit. It is made up of two parts; the 'guarantee credit' for those aged 60 and over and the 'savings credit' paid to those age 65 or over. You may be eligible for both parts. To find further information and to get an application form, you can either visit the Pension Service website or telephone their helpline (see help list). They can arrange for somebody to visit you at home to support you in filling the form in or it may be completed over the telephone.

Tax Credits

Working Tax Credit (WTC) is a benefit that helps to top up low incomes. You may be eligible to claim this if you work 16 hours or more a week and are registered as partially sighted. The amount that you get depends on various factors, including the number of hours that you work, how many children you have and childcare costs.

Child Tax Credit (CTC) can be awarded to those with children whether they are in employment or not. If it is your child who is registered as having sight loss, you will qualify for a higher rate.

Your local Jobcentre Plus can give you further information and an application form about tax credits or you can telephone the Tax Credit helpline on 0845 300 3900.

Grants

Grants are another way of sourcing money to fund essentials. There are a number of different grants that you may wish to consider.

Your local social care department

Contact your local social care department to ask them if there are any grants available locally. They can sometimes help to identify funding for specialist equipment to make life easier or fees towards a residential home or respite care.

RNIB grants

RNIB offers grants to help with the daily life of people with sight loss. These grants are means tested and are intended for those on a low income and with savings of less than £10,000.

Grants may be given for household equipment such as washing machines and furniture. RNIB also considers grants for specialist reading equipment, essential adaptations, holidays and other domestic equipment.

The Social Fund

If you are on a low income and are faced with financial difficulties, you may be able to apply to the Social Fund. The fund can give a payment, grant or loan to individuals to fund things such as heating costs during cold weather, clothing or footwear and items for the home. Your local Jobcentre Plus will be able to provide you with an application form or you can download one from Directgov.

Local charities

If you have a specific piece of equipment in mind that you would like to purchase, you may wish to approach a local charity to fundraise on your behalf. The Rotary Club or the local Lions Club are usually keen to help a good cause.

Additional financial help

If you are registered as severely sight impaired, you are able to access a number of schemes that will save you money. You will qualify for:

* Free NHS sight tests.

* A 50% reduction on the cost of your TV licence – you should contact the TV licensing agency for further information (see help list).

* Free postage on items marked 'articles for the blind'.

* Blind Person's Income Tax Allowance – further details about this allowance can be found from contacting your local tax office.

* The British Wireless for the Blind Fund may be able to supply you with a free radio (see help list).

* Your social worker can apply to a charity called 'Telephones for the Blind' (see help list) in order for you to gain some financial support around your quarterly bills or for line installation. Criteria are in place for applications and it would be advisable to speak to your social care department who can support you in making an application.

* You may also be entitled to car parking concessions under the Blue Badge Scheme. This applies even if someone else drives the car (see help list).

In addition to these benefits, you may also be able to apply for the following.

* Reductions in admission costs at local attractions such as museums or leisure clubs. If you need a personal assistant or carer, enquire about whether they can accompany you free of charge. You may be asked to provide proof of your sight loss, so check before you travel if any identification is needed.

'If you are registered as severely sight impaired, you are able to access a number of schemes that will save you money.'

- A Disabled Person's Railcard which will help you to enjoy rail travel at a discounted rate. Contact your local railway station for further information or the National Rail Enquiries (see help list).

- Often local councils will have travel schemes that you may be able to access for a reduced cost. Contact them to find out what is on offer in your area.

- You can apply for a free Direct Enquiries service from BT even if they are not your telephone provider. To do this simply dial 195 and request exemption from the charges.

Dealing with debt

You may be worried about debt or costs spiralling out of control. This isn't something that should be ignored – this is the worst thing you can do. There are a lot of charities and resources out there providing free debt advice, but don't be fooled into using debt management companies that charge you a fee.

Debt Advice Foundation

The Debt Advice Foundation is a registered charity that provides free and impartial advice to those in debt (see help list). They will help you find free solutions to your difficulties; often the first step to sorting out your debt problems is by acknowledging and talking about them.

Face-to-Face

RNIB and Citizens Advice Bureau have teamed up to provide those with sight loss face-to-face support around debt management. If you or somebody you know has sight difficulties and is worrying about money, it may be helpful for them to speak to a Face-to-Face advisor. The scheme is currently running in 10 locations across England. Contact your local Citizens Advice Bureau to find out if there is a service in your local area.

Sight loss and employment

If you are looking for a job or want help to stay in employment, read on for simple-to-follow advice and tips.

Job hunting

It may be that you have been out of work for some time and are now looking to get back into the workplace. Action for Blind People has employment advisors who can support you to find work. They will be able to work with you on a one-to-one basis in order to ensure that you are prepared to go back into the workplace. Workstep is a Jobcentre Plus initiative that encourages disabled people to find work. Action for Blind People is a provider of Workstep and aims to help individuals overcome barriers to employment. To find out more about these schemes, contact Action for Blind People (see help list).

The Disability Discrimination Act of 1995 ensures that people with a disability are not discriminated against when it comes to recruitment and selection for employment. The Act also states that an employer should make changes to help a person at work. You should always fill in application forms honestly and make the employer aware of your sight difficulties at this stage.

Staying in work

Many people believe that once their sight begins to deteriorate that they have no alternative other than to give up work. This is not the case – there is support that you can access. The government's Access to Work scheme can help you to stay in employment by giving you and your employer advice and assistance with additional costs that may be incurred due to your sight loss. Details of this scheme can be found by contacting your local Jobcentre Plus or visiting the Directgov website.

'Action for Blind People have employment advisors who can support you to find work. They will be able to work with you on a one-to-one basis in order to ensure that you are prepared to go back into the workplace.'

If you are finding your role challenging due to your sight loss, you may wish to consider what changes are needed to make things easier. Write a list of the things that you find difficult and possible solutions. Complete the table with issues that you feel need considering at work. For example:

Problem	Possible Solution
In winter the lighting in the office is too dim	To use a desk lamp
I can't read the company news bulletin as the print is too small	Increase the font size of the print

Writing down your difficulties will help you to consider possible solutions. It will also be helpful for when you speak to your employer so that you can offer them guidance around how they can meet your needs.

Self-employment

One option that you may not have considered if you are struggling with work is to become self-employed. Running your own business can be very hard work but also immensely rewarding. You would need to consider your strengths and skills carefully in order to decide what sort of business you could set up. Action for Blind People has a network of self-employment advisors who you can contact for further advice and support.

Quick action checklist

- Check that you are receiving your benefit entitlement by contacting the RNIB helpline.

- Contact your local authority to find out if they offer any reduction in travel or entrance fees to local attractions.

- Discuss any debt problems with a debt advisor.

- Don't shy away from investigating employment opportunities.

Summing Up

- If money is causing you concern, you need to check that you are claiming everything you're entitled to. Debt can cause a great deal of stress and it is important to do something about it before it mounts up any further.

- If you are struggling at work, you need to consider how you can make life easier. Share your concerns with your employer; they are obliged to accommodate your needs to make sure that you can carry out your duties effectively.

- If you are considering finding work or setting up your own business, seek advice from one of Action for Blind People's employment advisors.

Chapter Ten

Sight Loss with Other Disabilities

Sometimes sight loss can be accompanied by other disabilities. You may have mobility problems or other sensory impairments such as a hearing difficulty. Others may have learning difficulties or have experienced a stroke. In this chapter we will explore other disabilities that may accompany sight loss. This chapter will:

- Help you to identify where you can turn to for support.

- Offer advice on how to make daily life easier when you have a dual disability.

Sight loss and mobility difficulties

If you have mobility difficulties and start to lose your sight, it can make getting around doubly difficult.

If you have a social worker, you may wish to ask them about what support is on offer in your local authority. Alternatively, you should mention your difficulties to your GP who can arrange for an assessment of your needs to take place.

Wearing protective eye wear when outside can help with the glare of UV rays and help to increase your mobility. RNIB has a selection of eye shields to choose from and can offer advice on selecting the right pair for your needs.

An occupational therapist, or OT as they are often referred to, can help you by giving advice on how your home or workplace should be adapted to manage your mobility difficulties. For example, if you use a wheelchair they will be able to arrange for ramps to be fitted.

'Alternatively, you should mention your difficulties to your GP who can arrange for an assessment of your needs to take place.'

If you have sight loss and a mobility difficulty, managing around the home can be challenging. An OT can assess you in your home and advise what equipment might help to make life easier. For example, if you are finding washing increasingly difficult, they may be able to supply you with a bath seat or perching stool, or grab rails could be fitted around the home for you to hold onto for additional stability.

Sometimes the OT will be able to suggest new ways of doing things that will help to increase your mobility. For example, if you find that stamina is a problem they may be able to show you different ways of doing your daily activities to help conserve some energy.

A physiotherapist can assess your mobility to decide whether you need a walking frame or any other mobility equipment. They may also suggest exercises that you can carry out to improve your mobility.

Referrals to both the occupational therapy department and physiotherapist can be done via your GP.

If you choose to use a walking stick to support your mobility, you should ensure that an occupational therapist or physiotherapist assesses you to make sure that the stick is the correct height. You can use a ferrule, the rubber attachment at the very bottom of a walking stick, to give you greater stability and support – this can be particularly helpful if you are walking on uneven surfaces. You may wish to use white tape on your walking stick to indicate your visual problems. Some white tape is also reflective so is particularly useful if you are heading out at night.

Sometimes it is necessary to consider using a wheelchair. Your GP can refer you to the NHS wheelchair service and they can arrange for an assessment to take place. The British Red Cross has a wheelchair lending service. You can borrow a wheelchair for up to six weeks but you will need a letter from your GP to state your needs (see help list).

Sight loss and hearing impairment

We rely heavily on what we see and hear in order to make sense of the world and when hearing and sight loss are combined, life can seem very challenging. If you suspect your hearing is not as good as it might be, but you have not seen anyone about it, it is important to get your hearing checked so that you can get the correct level of support. Make an appointment to discuss your concerns about your hearing levels with your GP.

Your GP can arrange for a hearing test to take place at your local audiology department and you may be able to be fitted with a hearing aid. You should also ask at your appointment whether there is access to a rehabilitation officer or similar professional as they may be able to offer you the practical and emotional support that you need. In some areas there are specialist officers too.

If you are found to have hearing difficulties, you may be registered as either:

■ Hard of hearing – uses a hearing aid.

■ Deaf – uses signing/writing.

■ Deaf – uses lip reading/speech.

Your local authority may be able to provide support after an assessment of your needs – you should contact your social worker for more information.

Deafblind UK is a national charity that aims to support those with vision and hearing loss. The charity aims to help those affected to remain as independent as possible, maintain their quality of life and reduce feelings of isolation. RNID also offers support (see help list).

Sight loss and learning disability

It is estimated that over 1.3 million people in the UK have a learning disability, and around 1 in 3 will have sight problems. If you are caring for someone with learning difficulties, bear in mind they might find it hard to explain their sight problems so these could quite easily go undetected. Changes in behaviour could be an indication that they're having problems with their sight. They may:

■ Become withdrawn and depressed.

■ Find it more difficult to do everyday things.

■ Stop wanting to go out.

■ Stop moving around their home.

It is important that anyone experiencing sight loss alongside learning difficulties accesses the correct support – rehabilitation officers are the best people to go to for help.

It is crucial that anyone with learning difficulties understands what is happening to their sight and that they are fully supported to adapt. LookUp is a website that aims to provide information about eye care to those who support individuals with a learning difficulty (see help list). Factsheets have been produced that aim to be easier for those with learning difficulties to access.

Sight loss and strokes

Strokes can happen to anybody, but generally occur in those over the age of 65. It is estimated that 150,000 people have a stroke in the UK every year. The effects of a stroke depend on which part of the brain is deprived of oxygen; sight loss most commonly occurs in those that have a stroke in the right side of the brain.

When a person has a stroke, vision can be affected in a number of ways including:

- Partial sight loss.
- Difficulties judging visual depth.
- Loss of visual field.
- Double vision.
- Sensitivity to light.
- Problems with eye muscles.

You can find it hard to get to grips with sight problems alongside other problems caused by a stroke. An ophthalmologist will assess your visual problems and a team of health specialists can be involved in the rehabilitation process.

The Stroke Association is a UK-wide charity that offers support to those who have experienced a stroke, as well as their carers. The website has a forum where you can share your experiences with others, a helpline and a range of factsheets (see help list).

Advice for carers

Experiencing sight loss alongside other disabilities creates a complex situation where care and resources may be coming from several different sources. You should:

- Help and encourage the person in your care to access the correct resources for their disability – either through their GP, the local authority's social care department or any of the charities mentioned here.

- You should also access support for yourself. It can be exhausting being a carer and it's vital that you look after yourself in order to continue providing a good level of care for your loved one.

Quick action checklist

- Check the organisations and charities mentioned in this chapter to access specialist advice about your condition.

- Contact your social worker to see if they are able to offer you any additional support or resources.

- Contact your GP to make them aware of your additional needs.

Summing Up

Having an additional disability on top of sight loss can mean that life can be extremely challenging. Finding organisations that understand your situation and provide a space for sharing with others going through similar experiences may help to reduce your feelings of isolation. If you are finding life challenging, visit your GP and ask for an assessment of your additional needs.

Help List

Voluntary organisations and helplines

Action for Blind People

14-16 Verney Road, London, SE16 3DZ
Tel: 0303 123 9999 (helpline)
helpline@rnib.org.uk
www.actionforblindpeople.org.uk
Action for Blind People runs a free information and advice service and can advise on many issues associated with visual impairment.

Age UK

York House, 207-221 Pentonville Road, London, N1 9UZ
Tel: 0800 169 8787 (helpline)
www.ageuk.org.uk
Age UK is the amalgamation of Age Concern and Help the Aged. It provides information sheets and factsheets covering a number of subjects which affect older people.

British Red Cross

UK Office, 44 Moorfields, London, EC2Y 9AL
Tel: 0844 871 11 11
www.redcross.org.uk
British Red Cross provides short-term support to vulnerable people in the UK, whether they're recovering from an operation, need a wheelchair or just need help coping around the house. For information on how to access the services, visit the 'near you' section of the website or call the switchboard number listed above.

British Wireless for the Blind

10 Albion Place, Maidstone, Kent, ME14 5DZ
Tel: 01622 754757
www.blind.org.uk
British Wireless for the Blind supplies radio and audio sets to all registered blind and partially sighted people who are in need.

Deafblind UK

National Centre for Deafblindness, John and Lucille van Geest Place, Cygnet Road, Hampton, Peterborough, PE7 8FD
Tel: 0800 132 320 (helpline)
www.deafblind.org.uk
Deafblind UK is a charity offering specialist services and support to deafblind people.

Diabetes UK

Macleod House, 10 Parkway, London, NW1 7AA
Tel: 0845 120 2960 (helpline)
www.diabetes.org.uk
Diabetes UK run a range of support services including telephone counselling and local support groups. They also produce factsheets and information sheets on diabetes.

Guide Dogs

Burghfield Common, Reading, RG7 3YG
Tel: 0118 983 5555
guidedogs@guidedogs.org.uk
www.guidedogs.org.uk
Provides mobility and freedom to blind and partially sighted people. Guide Dogs for the Blind Association also campaigns for the rights of people with visual impairment, educates the public about eye care and funds eye disease research.

Hearing Concern Link

The Resource Centre, 356 Holloway Road, London, N7 6PA
Tel: 01323 638230 (helpline)
Textphone: 01323 739998
info@hearingconcernlink.org
www.hearingconcernlink.org
Hearing Concern Link provides advice and information to people affected by hearing loss.

Insight Radio

www.insightradio.co.uk
Run by RNIB, Insight Radio is the first radio station dedicated to blind or partially sighted people. Also available on Sky channel 0188 and freesat channel 777.

International Glaucoma Association (IGA)

Woodcote House, 15 Highpoint Business Village, Henwood, Kent, TN24 8DH
Tel: 01233 648 170 (helpline)
www.glaucoma-assocation.com
The IGA supports patients by providing information so they can co-operate fully in their treatment and prevent sight loss. It also promotes awareness and early detection of glaucoma, and supports and carries out research.

LookUp

Tel: 01372 755000
info@lookupinfo.org
www.lookupinfo.org
LookUp info is an information service on eye care and vision for people with learning disabilities from SeeAbility.

Macular Disease Society

PO Box 1870, Andover, SP10 9AD
Tel: 01264 350551
info@maculardisease.org
www.maculardisease.org
Charity aiming to build confidence and independence for those with central vision impairment. The only UK charity dedicated to helping people with macular degeneration.

The Partially Sighted Society

Queen's Road, Doncaster, DN1 2NX
Tel: 0844 477 4966
info@partsight.org.uk
www.partsight.org.uk
The Partially Sighted Society provides information, advice, equipment and clear print material for people with a visual impairment to help them make the best use of their remaining sight.

RNIB

105 Judd Street, London, WC1H 9NE
Tel: 0303 123 9999 (helpline)
www.rnib.org.uk
http://onlineshop.rnib.org.uk
RNIB provides a range of services, advice and information, including leaflets and publications, many of which are available in large print, Braille and Moon. They can also give details of local sight loss support organisations.

RNID

19-23 Featherstone Street, London, EC1Y 8SL
Tel: 0808 808 0123 (information line)
Textphone: 0808 808 9000
informationline@rnid.org.uk
www.rnid.org.uk

RNID is the charity working to create a world where deafness or hearing loss do not limit or determine opportunity, and where people value their hearing. It works by campaigning and lobbying, raising awareness of deafness and hearing loss, promoting hearing health, providing services and through social, medical and technical research.

Sense

101 Pentonville Road, London, N1 9LG
Tel: 0845 127 0060
Textphone: 0845 127 0062
info@sense.org.uk
www.sense.org.uk
Sense supports deafblind people throughout the UK, providing expert advice and information. The also provide holidays – have a look at the 'service' part of the website for more information.

The Stroke Association

Stroke House, 240 City Road, London, EC1V 2PR
Tel: 0303 3033 100 (helpline)
info@stroke.org.uk
www.stroke.org.uk
The Stroke Association provides community support in some areas and provides patient leaflets for people affected by stroke.

Telephones for the Blind

Tel: 01737 248032
www.tftb.org.uk
Telephones for the Blind provide telephones for the blind residents of the UK.

Health information and support

National Institute for Health and Clinical Excellence (NICE)

MidCity Place, 71 High Holborn, London, WC1V 6NA
Tel: 0845 003 7780
nice@nice.org.uk
www.nice.org.uk
NICE is an independent organisation responsible for providing national guidance on promoting good health and preventing and treating ill health.

National Screening Programme for Diabetic Retinopathy

www.retinalscreening.nhs.uk
The aim of the programme is to reduce the risk of sight loss amongst people with diabetes by the prompt identification and effective treatment, if necessary, of sight threatening diabetic retinopathy, at the appropriate stage during the disease process.

NHS Direct

Tel: 0845 4647
www.nhsdirect.nhs.uk
Call NHS Direct for health advice, open 24 hours a day, 365 days a year.

Smokefree

Tel: 0800 022 4 332
http://smokefree.nhs.uk
Call or visit the website for information and help to give up smoking.

Walking for Health (WFH)

Natural England, John Dower House, Crescent Place, Cheltenham, GL50 3RA
Tel: 0300 060 2287
wfhinfo@naturalengland.org.uk
www.whi.org.uk
Natural England's WFH encourages you to enjoy your local natural spaces and benefit your health by taking part in walks.

Holidays, travel and transport

Access at Last

18 Hazel Grove, Tarleton, Preston, Lancashire, PR4 6DQ
Tel: 01772 814 555
www.accessatlast.com
A one-stop-shop for accessible accommodation and services.

Blue Badge Scheme

www.direct.gov.uk
A scheme that allows holders of a blue badge to park for free in designated spaces. Click 'disabled people' then 'blue badge scheme' to find the relevant section of the website.

Disabled Persons Railcard

Rail Travel Made Easy, PO Box 11631, Laurencekirk, AB30 9AA
Tel: 0845 605 0525
disability@atoc.org
www.disabledpersons-railcard.co.uk
If you have a disability which makes travelling difficult, you get a third off most rail fares in the UK.

Driver and Vehicle Licensing Agency (DVLA)

Driver's Customer Services, Correspondence Team DVLA, Swansea, SA6 7JL
Tel: 0870 240 0009
www.dft.gov.uk
The DVLA should be informed if you have sight problems – use the contact details above to inform them of any changes in your sight that might have an effect on your ability to drive.

National Rail Enquiries

Tel: 08457 48 49 50
www.nationalrail.co.uk
Find information on travelling by train in the UK.

Torch Holiday and Retreat Centre

4 Hassocks Road, Hurstpierpoint, West Sussex, BN6 9QN
Tel: 01273 832282
TorchHRC@torchtrust.org
www.torchtrust.org
Torch Holiday and Retreat Centre is a Christian organisation providing specially designed holidays for partially sighted people.

Traveleyes

PO Box 511, Leeds. LS5 3JT
Tel: 0844 8040 221
www.traveleyes-international.com
Traveleyes provides accessible and adventurous holidays for visually impaired people.

Vision Hotels

14-16 Verney Road, London, SE16 3DZ
enquiries@visionhotels.co.uk
www.visionhotels.co.uk
Vision Hotels are a group of hotels offered through Action for Blind People to provide services and activities tailored to visually impaired people.

VisionOutdoor

Kassel e.V., Sachsenstr. 11, 34131 Kassel, Germany
Tel. +49 561 9223 459
info@visionoutdoor.de
www.visionoutdoor.de
Specialist holidays for visually impaired people.

Vitalise

www.vitalise.org.uk
Short breaks and respite care for disabled people.

Finance and benefits

Benefit Enquiry Line (UK)

Red Rose House, Lancaster Road, Preston, Lancashire, PR1 1HB
Tel: 0800 882 200 (helpline: Monday to Friday, 8.30am-6.30pm,
Saturday, 9am-1pm)
BEL-Customer-Services@dwp.gsi.gov.uk
www.direct.gov.uk/disability-money
Provides general advice and information for disabled people and carers on the
range of benefits available.

Citizens Advice Bureau (CAB)

www.citizensadvice.org.uk
With branches all over the country, the CAB offers free advice on finance and
legal matters. Visit the website to locate your local branch.

Debt Advice Foundation

Tel: 0800 043 40 50
www.debtadvicefoundation.org
A specialist debt charity offering free and confidential advice.

Directgov

www.direct.gov.uk
The UK government's digital service for people in England and Wales, with
information and practical advice about public services.

Jobcentre Plus

www.jobcentreplus.gov.uk
Provides information on looking for a job and claiming and making changes to
benefits.

Pension Service

Tel: 0800 991 1234 (helpline)
www.dwp.gov.uk
Contact to find out if you're eligible to claim Pension Credit.

Tax Credit Helpline

Tel: 0845 300 3900
Use this helpline number to find out if you qualify for any Tax Credits.

TV Licensing

Tel: 0844 800 5875 (helpline)
www.tvlicensing.co.uk
Check the website for the most up-to-date costs of a TV licence, if you're blind
you qualify for a 50% discount.

Need - 2 - Know

Available Titles Include ...

Allergies A Parent's Guide
ISBN 978-1-86144-064-8 £8.99

Autism A Parent's Guide
ISBN 978-1-86144-069-3 £8.99

Blood Pressure The Essential Guide
ISBN 978-1-86144-067-9 £8.99

Dyslexia and Other Learning Difficulties
A Parent's Guide ISBN 978-1-86144-042-6 £8.99

Bullying A Parent's Guide
ISBN 978-1-86144-044-0 £8.99

Epilepsy The Essential Guide
ISBN 978-1-86144-063-1 £8.99

Your First Pregnancy The Essential Guide
ISBN 978-1-86144-066-2 £8.99

Gap Years The Essential Guide
ISBN 978-1-86144-079-2 £8.99

Secondary School A Parent's Guide
ISBN 978-1-86144-093-8 £9.99

Primary School A Parent's Guide
ISBN 978-1-86144-088-4 £9.99

Applying to University The Essential Guide
ISBN 978-1-86144-052-5 £8.99

ADHD The Essential Guide
ISBN 978-1-86144-060-0 £8.99

Student Cookbook – Healthy Eating The Essential Guide
ISBN 978-1-86144-069-3 £8.99

Multiple Sclerosis The Essential Guide
ISBN 978-1-86144-086-0 £8.99

Coeliac Disease The Essential Guide
ISBN 978-1-86144-087-7 £9.99

Special Educational Needs A Parent's Guide
ISBN 978-1-86144-116-4 £9.99

The Pill An Essential Guide
ISBN 978-1-86144-058-7 £8.99

University A Survival Guide
ISBN 978-1-86144-072-3 £8.99

View the full range at **www.need2knowbooks.co.uk**.
To order our titles call **01733 898103**, email **sales@ n2kbooks.com** or visit the website. Selected ebooks available online.

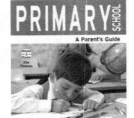

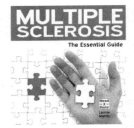

Need - 2 - Know, Remus House, Coltsfoot Drive, Peterborough, PE2 9JX